Shane Stark has made a career out of not having a career. Despite an early obsession with the bass guitar, he never made it to rock star, unless you count making it to the Australian Air Guitar finals two years running. Seriously. Among other vocations, he has been a stock boy, bartender, bush regenerator, semi-professional poker player, government pen pusher and (not very) Able Seaman in the Royal Australian Navy. He has also tried his hand at acting and stand-up comedy. He currently owns and runs a small vinyl record shop in Canberra, Australia. His family and friends have bugged him for ages to write a book. He hopes this first attempt will keep them happy.

Might As Well Be Me

Shane Stark

Might As Well Be Me

Vanguard Press

VANGUARD PAPERBACK

© Copyright 2023
Shane Stark

The right of Shane Stark to be identified as author of
this work has been asserted by him in accordance with the
Copyright, Designs and Patents Act 1988.

All Rights Reserved

No reproduction, copy or transmission of this publication
may be made without written permission.
No paragraph of this publication may be reproduced,
copied or transmitted save with the written permission of the
publisher, or in accordance with the provisions
of the Copyright Act 1956 (as amended).

Any person who commits any unauthorised act in relation to
this publication may be liable to criminal
prosecution and civil claims for damages.

A CIP catalogue record for this title is
available from the British Library.

ISBN 978 1 80016 628 8

*Vanguard Press is an imprint of
Pegasus Elliot Mackenzie Publishers Ltd.*
www.pegasuspublishers.com

First Published in 2023

**Vanguard Press
Sheraton House Castle Park
Cambridge England**

Printed & Bound in Great Britain

A big thank you to every musician responsible for the creation of the albums referenced in this book. The amazing, bizarre, unbelievable, and (mostly) happy memories that each album generated will be with me forever. Thanks to my good friend Margaret Dowel, the grooviest ex-English teacher I know, for her brilliant editing and feedback. It was appreciated more than she knows. I would also like to thank every family member, friend, work colleague and stranger who has enjoyed my written ramblings and musings over the years. Your feedback, encouragement and (let's face it) pestering, are the reason this book (finally) exists. Finally, I would like to thank my soul sister, Tammy Mead. I honestly don't know where I'd be without you.

For Craig
(17.03.1976 – 27.03.2020)

"I've found that no matter what life throws at me, music softens the blow."
— Bryce Anderson

"Without music, life would be a mistake."
— Friedrich Nietzsche

"Music should be an essential part of any analysis."
— Carl Jung

"Music is the art which is most nigh to tears and memory."
— Oscar Wilde

Contents

Record/Chapter 1 15
Record/Chapter 2 18
Record/Chapter 3 21
Record/Chapter 4 24
Record/Chapter 5 26
Record/Chapter 6 29
Record/Chapter 7 32
Record/Chapter 8 35
Record/Chapter 9 37
Record/Chapter 10 40
Record/Chapter 11 43
Record/Chapter 12 46
Record/Chapter 13 48
Record/Chapter 14 51
Record/Chapter 15 54
Record/Chapter 16 56
Record/Chapter 17 61
Record/Chapter 18 64
Record/Chapter 19 67
Record/Chapter 20 70
Record/Chapter 21 72
Record/Chapter 22 75
Record/Chapter 23 78
Record/Chapter 24 81
Record/Chapter 25 84
Record/Chapter 26 87
Record/Chapter 27 89

Record/Chapter 28 91
Record/Chapter 29 93
Record/Chapter 30 96
Record/Chapter 31 99
Record/Chapter 32 101
Record/Chapter 33 104
Record/Chapter 34 106
Record/Chapter 35 108
Record/Chapter 36 112
Record/Chapter 37 114
Record/Chapter 38 117
Record/Chapter 39 120
Record/Chapter 40 122
Record/Chapter 41 124
Record/Chapter 42 126
Record/Chapter 43 128
Record/Chapter 44 130
Record/Chapter 45 132
Record/Chapter 46 134
Record/Chapter 47 136
Record/Chapter 48 138
Record/Chapter 49 140
Record/Chapter 50 142

Record/Chapter 1

Bon Jovi — Slippery When Wet (1986)

Puberty Blues At The Golden Arches

1987 was the year I became a man. Not in terms of sexual conquests, that wouldn't happen for months (maybe fact-check that); more in terms of sprouting hair in weird and wonderful places and earning enough money to buy my own music cassette tapes on a weekly basis. At fifteen, like many of my poorer peers, I was sent away for a two-year term at the golden arches, making and eating Quarter Pounders and not doing my cystic acne any favours.

Being a typically clumsy teen and with the attention span of a goldfish, I arrived at my first paid job with a Frank Spencer-like ability to initially fuck things up.

This included attempting to make pancakes with thick shake mix and nearly lopping a finger off twice on the same air vent. Nevertheless, I earned my gold star for burger flipping in record time.

I tried to maintain an air of authority standing behind the burger chute, doing my best, and mostly failing, to avert my eyes from the sublime body of register operator and surfer girl Nikki. I wasn't alone. Whenever she was on shift, restaurant efficiency somehow plummeted as half a dozen giggling and easily distracted pubescent boys struggled to load and fire their mustard canisters in accordance with store procedure. If you were a customer and received a cheeseburger that looked like it had just lost a fight, you could be pretty sure Nikki was working the till. Our manager, Bruce, an overtly gay guy in three-inch heels with Ken doll hair, would snap us out of our teenage stupor, usually by slapping us on the bottom and telling us to put our shoulders to the wheel. The encouraging bottom slap would fall out of favour in workplaces (including strip clubs) by the mid '90s. Sigh…

After closing, we would pump Bon Jovi's *Slippery When Wet* at eight on the volume knob of our grease-coated ghetto blaster as we cleaned and ingested as much food as we could handle. While Jon Bon Jovi sang 'Wanted Dead Or Alive', I fantasised about Nikki slipping into… well, anything but a Maccas uniform, mounting my hog and cruising around the city like Andrew McCarthy and Kim Cattrall in *Mannequin*. Fuck I miss the '80s.

Record/Chapter 2

Tone Loc — Loc'ed After Dark (1989)

(Not Very) Down With The Homies

At eighteen, I must have thought I was some sort of Renaissance man when I sat this super smooth hip-hop/street rap gem alongside Bon Jovi's *Slippery When Wet* and *The Best of Sergio Mendes and Brasil '66* in my record collection. Like most impressionable young white Australian males in 1989, this album was my first foray into the hip-hop genre. I thought Tone Loc was the second coolest guy on the planet; only pipped by Jerry Everett, the American import who played for the Newcastle Falcons in the 1980s Australian National Basketball League. Jerry was so freakin' cool, if he played in the American NBA, would have made

Michael Jordan look like a nerd on the court. But I digress…

Unlike Tone Loc, the only thing I knew about cool in 1989 was how to spell it. I was a grade-A nerd who wore a blazer and sensible shoes to school. Voluntarily. Like most white guys, I didn't learn until well into the noughties how to do that crossover thing with my hands when listening to hip-hop; but even then, like most white guys, I probably shouldn't have. I'm sure Tone would have been disappointed to learn that I would be forty-seven before I would discover the delights of a good 'Cheeba'.

I spent many a night in the early 1990s at Sydney nightclubs, listening to 'Funky Cold Medina' while doing a wildly exaggerated white boy shuffle, complete with way out-of-time hip thrusting. I regularly dressed in acid wash jeans and a Hyper-colour T-shirt (if you're not familiar, these were the tees that changed colour with your body temperature; very 'fly on a white guy' in 1991). Hyper-colour undies were also donned, twenty-year-old me being ever hopeful of a saucy show-and-tell moment that would never arrive, being blessed as I was with a rake thin physique and violent acne. A Southern Comfort and Coke in each hand completed the look, but didn't do anything to help my groin coordination on the dance floor. Essentially any eye contact I made with a girl while Tone Loc sang about doing the 'Wild Thing' was met with genuine pity, if not outright disdain.

My moves would improve over the next twenty years, culminating in me competing in the national air guitar finals two years running (more on that later). Any disdain I get from girls nowadays is generally from those with their shit together who don't understand why a fifty-year-old man would get around in a Van Halen T-shirt (RIP Eddie), especially if he's single.

Record/Chapter 3

ZZ Top — El Loco (1981)

Working Class Man-Boy

My adult working 'career', for want of a better word, began with Grace Bros department store in Sydney's Northern suburbs. I somehow passed customer service training, despite getting pissed at lunchtime on the last day and urinating in the towel reserve because I was so drunk I forgot the way to the toilets (not my proudest moment). Karma intervened, however, when, on arrival at work the following Monday I was relegated from cashier to stock boy (a.k.a. shit kicker).

I spent my glorious late teen working days riding around the store using a pallet jack like a scooter, pretending to look busy filling shelves and catching forty winks by climbing high up in the bedding department reserve and falling asleep in a sea of pillows. I particularly liked lingering for way too long at the perfume counters, where I was obsessed with a girl called Stacey. She was about thirty-five and looked like she'd just stepped out of a Motley Crue video, complete with a tight white dress, white stockings and hooker lipstick. I even found her bogan accent strangely alluring.

Being clumsy by nature, I developed the unfortunate moniker of 'The Granny Killer', after injuring two grannies in separate serious accidents within two weeks. On the first occasion, I ran through the door of the loading dock at speed, smashing it into, and breaking the nose of Hazel, a sixty-five-year-old dear who worked in the Manchester department. The second incident saw me step backwards on the shop floor and accidentally trip over a poor eighty-year-old duck. I turned and watched in slow motion as she fell face forward like a plank of wood, hitting the tiles with a whack, her arms doing very little to soften the blow.

I became friends with Mary who ran the store PA system. After bribing her with shots of Baileys in her coffee, I convinced her to regularly let me play ZZ Top's *El Loco* album through the system at a volume not considered retail-appropriate. The other stock boys and I would then walk the floor in fits of giggles, listening to tracks like 'Tube Snake Boogie' and 'Pearl Necklace'. We hoped to spot a gasp of horror when the sexual innuendo twigged with one of the septuagenarians browsing the haberdashery department. I think the best we got was a few tisk-tisks or looks of mild confusion. I was, and still am, very easily amused. Of course, I had told Stacey from the perfume department about my ZZ Top hi jinx, and nearly passed out one day when she asked me what 'Tube Snake Boogie' meant while simultaneously winking at me.

Record/Chapter 4

Push Push — A Trillion Shades Of Happy (1992)

All Blacks, Bars and Strippers

I followed the family to Christchurch, New Zealand in 1992, scoring a bar job at the Cantabrian Tavern, run by ex-all-black rugby player Fergie McCormick. His first question to me was, 'Are you quick?' which I would later learn was a prerequisite not only for efficient bar service, but the ability to duck flying bar stools when bikers and rugby players came to blows. I was never that worried though, as any trouble would soon be taken care of by Fergie, who, at five foot seven and built like a brick shithouse, would simply pick up each offender with one hand and walk them out the door like he was taking out the trash (which he was essentially).

One day a local rugby club booked a function at the bar. I tried to act all nonchalant and continue serving drinks as two strippers emerged on the pub's stage with several props including a wine bottle and a banana. Why would they bring an empty wine bottle? I briefly thought, before the lights, their tops, and what was left of my innocence, went down to the sound of Push Push's song of the year, 'Trippin'. Some poor lad from the club who was having a birthday was dragged into the middle of the floor, and under what could only be deemed as mild protest, had things done to him that he might have enjoyed more in the privacy of his own bedroom than with a fifty strong cheer squad. I couldn't look at a banana for months after the event.

Kiwi funk/hard rockers Push Push's album *A Trillion Shades Of Happy* was on high rotation all year; a bit like New Zealand's answer to Ugly Kid Joe and heaps of fun. Their song 'Trippin' was playing at a nightclub one night where you could watch yourself dancing on a giant video screen. This was a defining moment in my life, as I realised that certain shaped humans (including myself) should never ever be seen dancing in public, unless therapy is provided to those who bear witness to this humanitarian crime.

Record/Chapter 5

The Cruel Sea — Three-Legged Dog (1995)

Channelling Tex

Like many in the crowd, I had no idea who Tex Perkins was when, in 1991, embarrassing as it is to admit, I turned up to see Transvision Vamp play at the Hordern Pavilion in Sydney. While I waited with bated breath to see Wendy James come on stage in next to nothing ('appear' is probably a better choice of word there), a tall gangly looking guy who resembled a shaved ape started chanting 'Weeendyyy', over and over in a deep baritone voice, prancing about the stage and daring the audience to boo him. We obliged with the booing of course, being completely oblivious to the fact we were watching one of the coolest acts in

Australian rock history, and the blooming of an Aussie rock/sex god. In case you're reading from the States, here is a musical equation you may not be familiar with: Iggy Pop + Jim Morrison + Johnny Cash = Tex Perkins. It's safe to say if I was gay, I would be all over Tex; my other two *strictly hypothetical* choices being Tom Selleck and... don't laugh... Michael J Fox.

Years later, after discovering The Cruel Sea's brilliant *Three-Legged Dog* is a fantastic album to make love to (whatever that is, thanks a lot scamdemic), I had two opportunities to try and channel Tex's sexual energy into my own dating life, by seeing him play two shows with the beautifully messy Beasts Of Bourbon. On each occasion, one band member would pass out on stage or come precariously close to doing so. Tex would kick them awake, and they would pick up again without missing a beat. Or they might have missed a few, but you wouldn't have known it. If you ever saw the Beasts play, you'd know what I mean.

Meanwhile, Tex would keep the crowd guessing: *was he high? annoyed? sad? confused? spoiling for a fight? horny? all of these things? Why did the girls love him so much?* Despite keeping copious notes, my attempts at keeping girls guessing 'Tex' style would, and still do, only make me look creepy, crazy or constipated. In the meantime, *Three-Legged Dog* sits next to my bed, waiting for a sexy, vivacious, intelligent but loopy female who finds animal balloon making (more on that later), and knowing every single line to the movie Mad Max (more on that later too), beyond sexy.

Record/Chapter 6

Green Day — Dookie (1994)

All At Sea In The Navy

I really don't know what prompted me to join the Royal Australian Navy in 1994. If pressured, I would probably say the romance of life on the sea, with a sexy uniform and a girl in every port. Three days into recruit school, however, I realised two things: a) at twenty-two I knew I still had time to be a rock star (at fifty I still think I do, though my therapist disagrees; the bloody nerve!). And b) I'd never been more homesick, and just wanted my mum (still happens on a regular basis; love you, Mum).

I endured twelve weeks of mild torture: sleep deprivation, jumping into freezing water in overalls, and having the shit scared out of me by an extremely psychologically unsound physical trainer (let's say, psychopath). He had a cruel sneer that I doubted even a mother could love, and a penchant for gift wrapping his poo and giving it to one of the female recruits on graduation night (I wish I was making that bit up). At several points I thought of going AWOL, catching a ferry to Tasmania, growing a beard and hiding in a treehouse for four years. I still might if this *New World Order/Illuminati* crap doesn't end soon.

Green Day's awesome album *Dookie* kept me sane as I scrubbed shower blocks on my hands and knees all weekend after being reprimanded for not ironing my pyjamas correctly. I subsequently became the best PJ ironer on the base, and charged the guys in my division $10 to iron theirs, often under torchlight after lights out. *Dookie* was also a nice distraction once I got to sea, especially on nightshift below decks where I was tasked with manning the super-duper 1950's technology sonar on the guided missile destroyer HMAS Brisbane. Our ship was advanced enough to shoot down most aircraft, but a submarine could have been sitting right under us, as all we could generally hear was whales and dolphins farting — and me sighing thinking of the valuable time I was wasting not getting laid or being a rock star. The same sigh is happening as you read this.

I learned pretty quickly that navy life really wasn't for me. Showering in treacherous seas and trying to keep your balance in half a foot of sea water while surrounded by a dozen other showering guys with their schlongs out might go down well with gay gents or NRL players, but the thought of this being part of my daily routine for the next twenty years I did find just a tad off-putting. But it wasn't just the potential for PTSD from twenty years of inadvertent schlong sightings. I had to get out as I wasn't really a team player. When asked to join the 'piss' fund, which would involve being constantly inebriated when not on duty to see even a reasonable return on investment, I gracefully declined. The truth was I preferred to see the sights and have coffee and scones. Funnily enough, I never got any takers.

Record/Chapter 7

Vanity 6 — self titled (1982)

Sun and Stupidity in Costa Rica

At forty-three, I took a voluntary redundancy from my public service job. With a bundle of cash, no commitments and little financial common sense, I headed to Costa Rica to chase waves and senoritas; not necessarily in that order.

I enrolled at a school that taught Spanish, surfing and yoga, quickly falling in love with my Spanish teacher and most of the female students. One day a local employed at the school butchered an endangered iguana on the school grounds and had it barbecuing in no time. A vegan American guy in our group was deeply offended by this. I agreed it was a shameful thing to do, and tried to be as discreet as I could as I chowed down on my first grilled iguana tail salad (pretty good actually, tastes like chicken).

On a bigger surf day, I did my best to impress the girls in my class by vertical dropping into twelve-foot waves and winning an impromptu push-up competition on the shore with the young surf instructors. Chest puffed out and head growing rapidly, I had visions of serenading the girls around the campfire later that evening like Elvis in *Blue Hawaii*, walking from one to the other as I sang and letting them know there's plenty of me to go around. My ego was somewhat deflated, however, after Miriam, a lovely young French girl in our group, had her teeth smashed in when her surfboard hit her square in the face as she went to pick it up near the shore. My consoling and manly arm around her shoulders lasted about thirty seconds before I passed out from the sight of her front teeth swinging like a gate in the bloody maw that used to be her pretty mouth.

After a week of surfing, I braved a few days in the capital San Jose, a mish-mash of modern and third-world cities, where endemic corruption meant you could walk out of a five-star hotel and fall into one of the hundreds of two-foot potholes which could be seen scattered up and down the streets like the holes in Swiss cheese.

On a thirty-five-degree day and desperate for beer, I wandered into the Del Rey Hotel and Casino. There were hot women everywhere, including a few on a stage dancing in a somewhat disinterested fashion to 'Nasty Girl' by Vanity 6. As I wasn't against the idea of falling in love with a feisty Latin American princess, I propped myself up at the bar and waited for the law of attraction to drop said princess into my lap. It was only fifteen minutes later, drink in hand, with a dozen scantily clad women surrounding my table, undressing me with their eyes and telling me what $100 could buy, that my sunburnt idiot brain realised I wouldn't be walking any of these hotties down the aisle… at least not without a solid down payment.

Record/Chapter 8

Del Amitri — Twisted (1995)

My Scottish Roots, part 1

I arrived in Edinburgh in September 1996, broke but keen to follow in the footsteps of my Scottish ancestors. After a night in a hostel room with no working windows that smelled so awful I figured at least one of the thirty-two guys in the room had to be dead, I hit the streets to try and find a job. I spent a week walking all over the city with my resume, the occasional local leaning out of a moving car to tell me to 'fuck off back home you Aussie prick', my olive skin and non-British teeth obviously a dead giveaway. In desperation, I briefly entertained the idea of becoming a male escort (I even drafted an ad for the local paper), before accepting that the horror of who I might be forced to make the beast with two backs with would fully outweigh any financial benefit I would obtain from such tawdry liaisons. I decided to trust the universe to look after me and choofed off around the country to pat some hairy cows.

I joined a small tour group led by Ian, a stocky red headed ex-soldier with a dodgy moustache. The first night we camped under the stars on the shores of Loch Ness. As hard as I tried to chat up the Eastern European girls by the campfire, Ian, who quickly got high as a kite, would keep interrupting us with war stories about blowing soldiers' heads off at close range in the Falklands. While this did sort of ruin the romantic ambience I was going for, I did manage a mild level of success, making out with Sara, a Dutch girl who shared a love of waffles and Scottish band Del Amitri. After a bit of drunken discussion about whose bottom was cuter, some dancing and a joint spew (haggis, beer and vodka was never going to end well), we settled into a sleeping bag to spoon for the night, listening to one of my favourite songs of all time, 'Driving With The Brakes On', from Del Amitri's brilliant album *Twisted*. The magic of the moment was lessened just a little by the mingling scents of Sara's Clinique Happy perfume and vomit, Ian's stoned ramblings through the night about AK47's, and the Loch Ness monster (or something just as freaky) moaning quite loudly out in the middle of the lake.

Record/Chapter 9

The Proclaimers — Sunshine On Leith (1988)

My Scottish Roots, part 2

I continued on my tour through the Scottish Highlands, carrying a bit of a cold after trying to impress everyone by jumping into ten-degree Glen Nevis in nothing but my Calvin Kleins. I got a kick out of stopping at Kyle of Lochalsh, where they were filming series three of the police show *Hamish Macbeth.* During a break in filming, I stood metres from actor Robert Carlyle in his police uniform as he smoked a cigarette and took in the sun. He looked like he really didn't want to be disturbed, but being a massive fan of his film *Trainspotting*, I couldn't help myself. I yelled out, "Robert! Do Begbie! Do Begbie!" He obliged (sort of), not by saying anything, but by sticking his ciggie in the side of his mouth and giving me an aggressive 'up yours' gesture. Made my week.

After the tour, I settled for a few months in the beautiful highland city of Inverness. I found a job selling phones and processing phone bills for British Telecom, wondering how long I could survive on £3 an hour, baked beans for dinner and hand washing my undies to save money at the laundromat. At night I worked at a Scottish themed bar where the pay was just as appalling and we all had to wear kilts.

The Proclaimer's song '500 Miles' from their album *Sunshine On Leith* had officially become Scotland's national song, pretty much like 'Down Under' for us Aussies. Some bozo would play '500 Miles' on the pub jukebox every bloody hour. It only became bearable after my workmates and I came back from our half-hour break pissed as newts, serving and singing along merrily, while (I'm glad to say) female after female kept wandering up to lift the Aussie's kilt and see if he was a true Scotsman (I was!).

I lived in a beautiful old guest house a few miles out of town that was known to be haunted. I would ride my bicycle home in the snow at one a.m. after my shift, slightly drunk and sliding all over the icy streets. On arriving home, stepping into the massive foyer was like stepping into a scene from *The Addams Family*. Two knights in shining armour greeted me, along with a zoo's worth of taxidermy animals including a full taxidermy lion. Trying not to shit myself, I would sprint to the huge spiral staircase thirty metres in the distance, trying to pretend I didn't hear the footsteps and voices I clearly heard behind me.

On the upside, living in the room next door to me was Jill, a sassy nightclub manager from Newcastle, England, who I fell in love with immediately. Her husky Geordie accent did terrible things to me. Our torrid affair would be regularly interrupted by the ghosts who would play with the pay phone in the hall, and cause Gary the 300-pound Star Trek nerd who lived in the attic room directly above us to scream like a little girl. One night at about two a.m. I heard '500 Miles' playing on what sounded like the gramophone player downstairs; the ghosts obviously being as just as annoyingly patriotic as the living.

Record/Chapter 10

Headlifter — Non Compos (1999)

Man About Sydney Town

In 1999 I entered the world of high finance… well, I exchanged foreign currency for tourists in Kings Cross. When I wasn't shooting the breeze with the Porky's strip club spruikers next door, I would gawk at the full gamut of humanity walking past. My favourite specimen was a mean-looking 250-pound behemoth of a cross-dresser who looked like the wrestler George 'The Animal' Steel in Doc Martens and a frilly house dress.

My supervisor Simon was a super funny gay guy who dressed like a GQ model. He also happened to be a heroin addict, which we all knew was the reason the till would be out on a regular basis. He sadly died from an overdose just a few weeks into our friendship. Fellow cashier Aaron helped to cheer me up. He was the last of the old school very un-politically correct pick-up artists. Being the shy young wallflower I was, I went out with him to 'learn the ropes'. I managed the cheeky smile and the wink across the room, but baulked at his slap on the bottom technique with a 'Who's your daddy, bad girl!' thrown in for good measure. Of course, nowadays he'd be hung, drawn and quartered, with witnesses to such flirting atrocities needing a safe space and a press conference to process what they'd just seen. But back then, besides the odd slap in the face, most girls just laughed, and on occasion he'd end up going home with one. Politically correct or not, I thought he was the master, so dragged him to live music gigs around Sydney with the hope of getting laid by association.

I really enjoyed taking him to see Nitocris, the Australian all-female metal act who I was a bit obsessed with at the time. I loved their grungy and sexy look, and would fantasise about becoming their roadie and doing all their 'dirty' work.

My obsession with the girls was diverted one evening by their supporting act, Sydney alt-metal band Headlifter. They blew the girls off the stage with one of the most hard-hitting, raw and powerful performances I'd ever seen. Their singer Caspian de Looze (now an artist to rock stars around the world), remains to this day one of the best frontmen I've ever witnessed. While I drooled over Headlifter and their punch-in-the-guts tracks from the album *Non Compos*, the girls from Nitocris drooled over Aaron after their set. The phrase 'it shoulda been me' would feature (and continues to feature) predominantly in my dating life. Applications still open at the time of writing:).

Record/Chapter 11

Suicidal Tendencies — Lights Camera Revolution (1990)

Flatmates (OR Arguments For Living Alone)

Flatmates have been the bane of my life for the last thirty years, along with many other banes, but let's go with flatmates for now.

The loopiest by far was a teacher called Karen. When not flooding the bathroom or setting the kitchen on fire, she would call me from random locations asking for a lift after running out of petrol. She was a special type of crazy and admitted to losing it sometimes in the classroom, having a meltdown and drawing on her face with a permanent marker in front of the kids. At the time I thought she was nuts; but then if I had to teach a bunch of woke kids whose extreme left-wing parents believe everything they see and read on social (ist) media, I'd probably end up doing the same.

Mark was a fairly harmless nerdy British guy, but at breakfast had this extremely annoying habit of slowly sliding his feet back and forth over my nice Berber carpet. I had regular visions of strangling him with a football sock.

Mohammed had a foot porn obsession, which I discovered after asking to borrow his computer and seeing a screensaver image that gave me post-traumatic stress disorder for a year.

James was an impeccably dressed and polite young man; a guy you'd want your daughter to meet. Until you discovered that leaving a feral pig in the room for six months would cause far less damage and destruction. Only a cleaner experienced in crime scenes was able to make the room look 'not horrific' again.

Ian was a grade-A moron who owned a hot pink worked Mitsubishi with 'SEX-UUP' number plates. He kept me awake with horrible hip-hop music and the smell of mediocre-quality marijuana into the early hours. The procession of very dumb but very hot girls passing through to his room made me sick and jealous in equal measure. On my departure, I let down all his tyres. It was the least I could do.

To help me cope with my flatmate woes, I would either stick forks in my legs, try to go to a happy place (usually involving a beach, Michelle Pfeiffer and some baby oil), or play 'You Can't Bring Me Down' from Suicidal Tendencies' brilliant album *Lights Camera Revolution*. When psycho Mike Muir said 'Tell 'em what's up Rocky!', the guitar solo that followed was like soup to my tortured soul.

Record/Chapter 12

The Verve — Urban Hymns (1997)

Culture Vulture

I arrived home from Scotland in early 1997, quickly realising that most Australian accents actually hurt my ears (including my own). Ignoring the fact I had no qualifications, no money, and no work experience outside of lifting boxes, pulling beers, and tying up Australian warships at port, I quickly set back off overseas on a mission to get 'cultured'. Why I chose Brighton England I have no fucking idea.

In a world before media-driven fear, completely unjustified mandates and arbitrarily imposed social distancing rules for flu strains with 99.98% survival rates, I worked in an Irish bar that was packed to the rafters every night. Every gamut of humanity would cruise into our establishment: bikers, chavs, spivs, punks and ladyboys to name a few. When not helping the bouncers to break up fights between guys in fluoro puffer jackets and slicked-down hair (a style I would try and emulate to horrible effect), I would be on my hands and knees picking up broken glass or mopping up vomit, sandwiched between 300 punters moshing to 'Bittersweet Symphony' from The Verve's album *Urban Hymns*. My vision of seducing French girls with the poetry of Keats and Shelley vanished in a haze of cigarette smoke as I sat huddled over after copping stray punches in the guts.

Yes, Brighton delivered culture of a different kind. A city with no shortage of weird and wonderful characters and one of the most diverse places in the United Kingdom. I was particularly impressed by a local guy called Michael who had achieved minor celebrity status. He was a huge black Dutch DJ, whose everyday car was a bright red Mack truck. He would cruise up and down the promenade with music pumping and his latest floozie by his side. If that wasn't enough, riding shotgun was Clive, his pet chimpanzee. Fuck culture I thought, this guy is the shit! At that point, I realised that no amount of art, literature or culture could cure my inner bogan, who, if offered the choice, would rather turn up for a first date in the Interceptor from *Mad Max* than in a Rolls Royce. One at a time ladies!

Record/Chapter 13

The Darkness — Permission To Land (2003)

A Year In The Tropics

In 2008, with several years under my belt as a government pen pusher/coffee imbiber, I took a year-long posting to the beautiful Solomon Islands.

Although a third-world country with its fair share of crime and cultural tension, mine was about as far from a hardship post as you could get. Indeed the most hardship I faced was on a weekly group jog through the long grass and waterways of local villages. I was shit-scared one of us would be taken by a crocodile; my only defence being a Walkman and a Journey — *Raised On Radio* CD.

Besides pushing pens, one of my daily tasks was to

drive coppers and soldiers back and forth between the base and the airport tarmac for their chopper flights. Security at the gate could only be described as 'casual'. A local copper sitting on a chair next to the gate (a long stick), would raise said gate with his foot and wave us through, checking vaguely that most of the people in the vehicle looked legit and weren't carrying bombs. My very unsettling bush beard was so bad that back home it would have warranted a body cavity search. It had to come off after I was reprimanded by the contingent commander for looking like serial killer Ivan Milat, which he supposed wasn't conducive to diplomatic relations.

On weekends we would crash the hotel pools in Honiara or take trips to some of the country's 980 islands. One weekend I flew to Gizo with my friend Julian. We stayed in a cabin over the water, agreeing that, while we liked each other, as we weren't gay or one of us female, it was somewhat of a waste. I also took a quick boat ride out to John F. Kennedy Island, where he was supposed to have beached his patrol boat during World War Two; just twenty years before his Illuminati colleagues had him knocked off.

To keep ourselves entertained on the base, we held a karaoke night prior to the monthly charter flight. I became famous for my rendition of 'I Believe In A Thing Called Love' by The Darkness. Not only could I hit the falsetto highs of Justin Hawkins (despite having no vocal range), I could kick higher than my head and owned the best mullet wig in the land. I would take the same act back to Canberra and become the oldest person in history to qualify for the Australian Air Guitar finals (more on that later). In the words of Metallica, 'Sad but true'.

Record/Chapter 14

Michael Jackson — Thriller (1982)

A (Non) Hat Trick In The Caribbean

In 2015, as part of my post-redundancy adventures, I booked a cruise for singles out of Miami, Florida. Having acquired a single cabin for a song, I had visions of middle-aged me shagging my way around the Caribbean for a week; which may have worked if the universe didn't conspire against me at every turn.

Immediately on boarding the ship, I fell in lust with Ola, a Russian fitness instructor from the U.S. Only I couldn't get near her all bloody week, as a creepy old bald guy (who looked like Peter Garret from Midnight Oil in leisurewear) was hanging around like a bad smell wherever she went. Although a pacifist by nature, I felt like bludgeoning him to death with his boat shoes.

I then turned my attention to Erica, a beautiful Latin American air hostess whose breasts entered the room about five seconds before she did. Just terrible. I had laid some fantastic groundwork, letting her teach me the Cuban salsa and some very rude Spanish vocabulary. But it all fell in a heap one day on Maho Beach on the island of Saint Martin. If you're not familiar, this is the beach where you can (for fun apparently) stand right behind the jet blast of a Boeing aircraft and enjoy the thrill of standing in a sand-filled wind tunnel with hundreds of other humans in swimsuits. I stood hand in hand with Erica on the beach, not for the first time in my life wondering what the hell I was doing, as a KLM 767 with its arse parked fifty metres in front of our faces hit the gas. I bravely let Erica's hand go and dropped to the ground in the foetal position, receiving an effective but extremely painful back exfoliation, as Erica was blinded by the sandstorm and adults and children ran around us screaming in pain. She spent the rest of the cruise at the sick bay nursing an eye infection as I threw profanities at the love gods for messing with my mojo yet again.

My last attempt was with Karen, a lovely natural-looking Canadian redhead with freckles. I spent an evening throwing my best Aussie charm at her. We kissed each other's faces off on the bow of the ship in true Titanic style, before she confessed to me she wasn't really looking for romance; partly as all three of her husbands had died on her.

"Oh, how awful, I'm so sorry," I said, trying to appear as nonchalant as I could as I quickly dumped my drink overboard and looked around for any sharp objects.

Having gone zero for three, I resigned myself to getting drunk and partying on the back deck disco on fancy dress night. Dressed as Virgil from my favourite childhood TV show *Thunderbirds*, I hopped on a raised platform in full view of the crowd and proceeded to gyrate to Michael Jackson's *Thriller*. Because that's what all single 43-year-old men do on boats in the middle of the Caribbean… right?

Record/Chapter 15

Europe — The Final Countdown (1986)

Swimming With (Card) Sharks

In 2009 I developed an unhealthy addiction to the game of Texas Hold'em Poker. Though I would eventually rank among the top tournament players in the country, I spent about six years blowing shitloads of cash while learning the ropes.

Not content to play at Canberra's excuse for a casino, I travelled interstate and eventually overseas to feed my addiction. I also dropped buckets of cash into online poker, a global scam only surpassed by Covid 19. I can safely say poker didn't do my dating life any favours. Most players were a variant of: a) hairy middle-aged middle eastern guys wearing Ed Harry T-shirts with questionable jewellery. Or b) androgenous Asian guys who were so slight they would break in half if they sneezed.

I did meet some interesting characters though. I played with tennis pros, Tour de France riders, famous actors and the odd known criminal. Perhaps my coolest poker encounter was in Los Angeles at the Commerce Casino, where I sat at a cash game table opposite the actor James Woods. Looking more like a grumpy alcoholic Santa Claus, you could tell that he still hadn't lived down starring in *The Hard Way* with Michael J Fox.

I also played against several poker professionals, soon realising that they're mostly no more talented than anyone else; they're just bankrolled by poker companies so able to develop a reputation for being scary and intimidating, with much of their good fortune stemming from other players playing mindbogglingly badly against them.

The pinnacle of my poker 'career' was reaching the final table of an Aussie Millions tournament in Melbourne. Self-conscious and sitting under unflattering spotlights, I didn't know what to be more embarrassed by, 'The Final Countdown' playing over the PA system, or cricketer bad boy Shane Warne announcing 'Shuffle up and deal!'

I still play now and then. If you sit down opposite a smug fifty-year-old silver fox with a perpetual four-day growth who looks like he spends too much time at the beach and wakes up at the crack of ten… it's probably me.

Record/Chapter 16

Motley Crue — Dr Feelgood (1989)

Life in cars

Being one of three boys, and with a petrol head for a father, I've experienced both the pleasure and pain of car worship.

My first car was a Datsun 200B that was more rust than car. I went to the country to crash the end-of-year-twelve parties for posh Sydney schools like Knox Grammar and Pymble Ladies College, regularly hitting 170kph on my P plates while my hungover friends napped in the back.

The family inherited my uncle Michael's Kombi van in 1982 after he fell asleep in it at the wheel and slammed into a telegraph pole head-on, dodging death by half a metre. My dad rescued her, performing a perfect 'cut and shut', turning two Kombis into one, and providing us with fun transport for our annual trip to Surfers Paradise to spend Christmas with the grandparents. We would set off at six p.m. for the (then) fourteen-hour trip up the (then) deadly Pacific Highway, me and my brothers sleeping on a mattress in the back and playing 'I Spy'. These trips began my lifelong love affair with the Australian muscle car, which in the early '80s could be spotted everywhere: Holden Monaro's, Ford Cobra's, and my dream car at the time, a lime green Sandman Panel Van!

My first foray into Aussie muscle car ownership came when I won a four-door V8 XC Ford Falcon at auction. A pine-lime-coloured beast, she hypnotized me with her highly worked-V8 engine and Mad Max-like blower. Before the auction I turned the engine over and just sat on the ground with my ear at the exhaust, drooling uncontrollably to the point where I started to get looks of concern. I knew I had to have her.

We lived in Guildford at the time (an Aboriginal word meaning the arsehole of Sydney). I would take her out to the brutalist industrial back streets, hitting ridiculous speeds while hoping the floaty steering and leaf suspension wouldn't suddenly give way; even Jeremy Clarkson would have been shitting himself.

On Saturday nights, full of testosterone and with no dating life to speak of, my mates and I would brush our mullets, dress up in our best flannelette shirts, acid wash jeans and belt buckles, and cruise the streets around Sydney Harbour looking for action. We would pull up outside some pumping nightclub, at which point I would crank up my Motley Crue *Dr Feelgood* cassette, get out of the car, light a cigarette and pretend to be a seasoned smoker as we walked around each other's cars and gushed over each other's 'donks'. I waited in vain for one of the many dream-like scenarios I had concocted in my head to materialise. The most favoured scenario would see the future Mrs Stark (preferably in the form of Claudia Karvan's character in the film *The Big Steal*), come out of a nightclub with her friends, who would dare her to walk up to me and ask me to show her how fast I could go.

Young, dumb, and full of cumbersome frustration at my involuntary long-term celibacy, I vented said frustration like any sensible twenty-two-year-old would; by drag racing and smoking my car up at the lights. When the cops finally pulled me over for dangerous driving and defected me for my bald ten-inch tyres, I tried to plead my innocence.

"I'm not like these other guys, officer! I'm a responsible and sensitive young man! I do origami! I took three-unit English at school! I can do cross-stitch for God's sake! I just like old Fords!" Of course, my pleading fell on deaf ears. Their 'if it quacks like a duck' smirks marked a turning point in my life; when I finally had to admit to myself that deep down, I really am at least part bogan. Sorry, Mum. VB anyone?

The following eighteen chapters are diary entries and observations I made that cover a period of five or six years, as my love for vinyl turned from a hobby into a full-blown obsession. Before somehow ending up with my own little record shop, I travelled up and down the East coast of Australia, desperately hunting down record collections and selling vinyl wherever and however I could. I had also become an expert in animal balloons, a hobby I randomly picked up while seeking distractions from a particularly stressful breakup. While most 'normal' guys in their forties were juggling families, mortgages and careers, I would be at various malls, markets and festivals, wearing a gigantic balloon cowboy hat and discussing the merits of eighties hair metal while simultaneously dealing with a queue of kids waiting with bated breath for a balloon puppy. The variety of humans I met along the way saw me laughing, crying, rolling my eyes or reeling in horror; often in the same day, if not the same hour. As with most of the stories in this book, names may be changed to protect the guilty, the innocent, or both.

Record/Chapter 17

Def Leppard — Hysteria (1987)

Vinyl on the Road, Series 1: The Batemans Bay Summer Slam, Episode 1

I rose at four a.m. after a restless five hours sleep, stressing about whether Henry (my car) would make the trip with a slow water leak. Praying to the God of the tragically single to give me just one (rhymes with ducking) break, I arrived weary but safe, and made a mental note to see a local mechanic in the morning, who I expected would tell me I have more chance of matching with Scarlett Johansson on eHarmony than getting my car looked at before the new year.

Before setting up my record stall, I waited an agonizing 15 minutes for my first coffee of the day and was fairly confident the teenage girl serving me wasn't genuinely sorry for the wait, despite my best attempt at looking like a fed up and world-weary middle-aged record dealer (my natural resting face actually). Not unexpectedly around the Christmas holidays, I noticed Batemans Bay's bogan per capita rate seemed to be outstripping Western Sydney by three to one. I was critical and jealous of their mega mullets in equal measure.

A loud self-confessed high functioning autistic guy made my ears bleed as he tried to convince me the copy of Whitesnake's *1987* I had for sale was the exact same one he used to own, as he could identify it by the scratches on the vinyl. The fact that my copy was in mint condition didn't seem to shake his conviction.

A young guy about sixteen was so excited to find a copy of Def Leppard's *Hysteria* he had to pull out his asthma inhaler to calm himself down. I could empathise, being as I am a lifelong Def Leppard tragic who has queued up for hours on three continents (once overnight in the snow) to see them play. He had a jacket with Iron Maiden, Dungeons and Dragons and unicorn patches. A bit confusing for the girls I thought, especially with his cherub face and blonde floppy hair. But at forty-eight, I still wished I was him.

Yummy mummies regularly wandered over to my stall during the day, partly to look at records, and partly to buy an animal balloon for their kids. Not for the first time I wondered: a) if I was the first person in history to sell vinyl and animal balloons at the same venue. And b) how the hell did I get here.

I felt very 'Bernard Black'-like for much of the day, as I had more borderline examples of humanity than I would have liked fingering my records, mostly with no intention of buying. One mouth breather walked past eating a bag of Cheezels. Badly. For a moment it looked like he might come over for a look, but I gave him a death stare that said I would disembowel him with a butter knife if he got within a metre. It seemed to work.

I arrived at my Airbnb, meeting my host Carole, a chain smoker with a gorgeous Jack Russell puppy called Jazz. Carole let me pig out on her Christmas leftovers while she chugged away on her Winfield Blue cigarettes in the living room and Jazz licked me silly (at the time of writing I remain on the lookout for a woman willing to do same). We reminisced on a bygone era when there were dances, people dressed up to go out, and hipsters would have been quite rightly ostracised from civil society.

Record/Chapter 18

Megadeth — Countdown To Extinction (1992)

Vinyl on the Road, Series 1: The Batemans Bay Summer Slam, Episode 2

I headed straight to the mechanic in the morning. As much as I would have liked the diagnosis to be a simple hose split, my heart sank as his soared with the announcement of 'water pump'. He smiled at me as he rubbed his hands together, leaving me in no doubt that he saw me coming, and was likely calculating in his head how much he could charge me without looking like he was taking the piss.

Sales were a bit slower, so I spent too much time watching mouth breathers with enough sugar in their shopping trolleys to start a diabetes epidemic in a small developing country. I saw one poor lass who had wingnut ears so wide she could have stood in the middle of a tinny and sailed. She'd passed the unfortunate trait to her two children. I had a vision of her in a pond with her kids swimming right behind her.

As I was making an animal balloon for a kid, a guy who looked about 120 years old approached my stall. He introduced himself as Hubert, a thirty-seven-year-long resident of Batemans Bay who originated from Austria. He motioned me closer as it seemed he had something important to say. For some reason I still can't fathom, he felt the urge to tell me there was a man shortage in Sydney. I could only surmise that perhaps he saw in me the look of the quietly desperate. He told me I'd do well with my balloons since they're nice and 'firm' (exact quote, I'm not kidding). Due to his age and the fact he looked and sounded quite sinister (well, at least capable of drowning a kitten), I assumed his childhood probably included a stint in the Hitler Youth. Of course, I was too afraid to ask him to confirm this, but in my imagination pictured him as an eight-year-old in what must have been a bizarre version of the Scouts, being asked to do mildly horrendous things for their badges.

Later I spent nearly an hour chatting to a guy who was the spitting image of the hyper nerdy cop from the *Police Academy* movies. In an episode of not judging a book by its cover, I was a little shocked to see him purchase Anthrax's *State Of Euphoria*, an album that can cause conniptions if you don't brace yourself. I was even more shocked to learn he was an ex-Battalion Commander in the U.S. Marine Corps with multiple tours of Afghanistan, Iraq and other war-torn countries. He told a sad story of keeping security for some elections and seeing a car full of people simply handing out how to vote leaflets being executed. They couldn't do anything as it was so crowded they couldn't get to the offenders before they lost them in the mayhem. He said he doesn't get on well with his sister because she calls him a baby killer. And I thought my family disagreements were bad.

I picked up my car in the afternoon; a gobsmacking bill as expected. I offered to part pay the mechanic with an original copy of Megadeth's *Countdown To Extinction* album but he wasn't having it. Yes, sadly there are some folks in this world who lack both compassion and good taste.

Record/Chapter 19

Bob Marley — Exodus (1977)

Vinyl on the Road, Series 1: The Batemans Bay Summer Slam, Episode 3

Before opening my stall, I went record hunting at Mogo (an Aboriginal word meaning highway bottleneck). I had time to kill so wandered into the local kitchen/homewares shop. I decided against buying a plastic banana protector on the basis that I'm still a man the last time I checked, and the purchase of said protector would surely be a sign that I've officially 'given up'. On leaving the shop, I passed a guy with a mangy beard and wearing socks with sandals in thirty-five-degree heat. I breathed a sigh of relief for passing on the banana protector, as I was pretty sure that guy owned one.

My first customer of the day was a guy who clearly hadn't seen a dentist since the Fraser administration. He regaled me for fifteen minutes with his toothless tale about seeing the Bob Marley *Exodus* tour at the Hordern Pavilion in Sydney. I didn't get much of the story as it was mostly delivered in vowels, but apparently Bob told the youngsters at the front to shut up or he wouldn't play. I didn't have the heart to tell him I couldn't sell any more records until he did the same.

Later I had fun entertaining a very smart little three-year-old girl who rocked up to my stall and started asking questions. Or at least her first dozen questions were fun, but I soon realised she wasn't going to stop asking questions… ever. I managed to explain to her what the Rolling Stones tongue means, and why Kiss are legends of rock (that was her exact question with no prompting), but after forty-five minutes of constant bombardment, I was hoping I would randomly pass out, and felt bad for wishing she would go home and stand on a piece of Lego.

I took a photo of my stall to stick up on Instagram. I tried to wait for a shot where the people crate digging didn't have a mullet, a singlet, sleeve tattoos, half their teeth missing or a trolley full of alcohol. It took a while I can tell you.

I went to a local club for dinner, bogan HQ but great food and views. There were lots of unhappy breeders feigning excitement over the seafood raffle. I felt sorry for one woman with tired drooping eyes who looked away from her family at me as if to say, 'What the fuck have I done?'

I ended my evening at the local ice cream parlour. The rum and raisin was almost better than sex... like I'd know.

Record/Chapter 20

The Barren Spinsters — Ten Steps To Cynical Thinking (2019)

Vinyl on the Road, Series 1: The Batemans Bay Summer Slam, Episode 4

After three nights of having the hostel cabin to myself, I had to share with three girls all under thirty. I'd like to say a wild night ensued and I was ravished to within an inch of my life, but the sexiest it got was me subjecting them to my dodgy hole ridden camouflage undies. Thankfully I have amazing legs from my kung fu practice, so I figured it sort of balanced out. I was sure I saw one of them surreptitiously bite her bottom lip; though I'll be first to admit my sex starved imagination has been known to play tricks.

Started my day chatting with a couple of funny old girls in their eighties who rocked up to my stall. We all agreed their generation had it great. They told me they're not afraid of the apocalypse or the power going out, because, unlike the current screen addicted generation, they know how to make a fire with sticks.

During a particularly slow stretch, I played a game I often do to help pass the time… doppelgänger spotting. It's surprisingly easier than you think. In half an hour I spotted a short fat Russell Crowe, twin Eddie Munsters, Benny Hill in Bali pants and the freaky headed guy from the movie *Weird Science.*

A smart-arse guy in leathers, seeing I had $45 on an original Motorhead album, asked me in a smart-arse tone how much I paid for it.

"None of your fucking business," I just managed not to say out loud. Record dealers are mostly friendly folk, but now and then you get a customer who you wish would walk into the ocean with a backpack full of spanners.

I was cheered up late in the day when I ran into a guy called Brendan, whose awesome blues/boogie rock band I'd seen perform in Canberra. They're called The Barren Spinsters. No irony here really, life just insists on throwing me reminders.

Record/Chapter 21

Col Hardy — Country (1978)

Vinyl on the Road, Series 2: The Country Bumpkin Hotpool Escape & Record Hunt, Episode 1

My first stop was Muswellbrook, where an old guy called Les with 1,500 records met me in town so I could follow him out to his property in the middle of bumfuck nowhere. I took in the beauty of the landscape as I sat behind his beat-up truck, his Pitbull giving me the evil eye as I pondered whether, on arrival at the property, I'd be hogtied at gunpoint and fed to the pigs.

I wasn't impressed when 1,499 records of the 1,500 turned out to be country and western. Still, I managed to find a couple of rare country gems, including *Country* by Aboriginal gentle giant of country soul Col

Hardy. I don't pretend to be crazy about country music, but you can't deny Col could carry off a pair of blinding white jeans better than most. It took me about an hour to sort through Les' collection, as he insisted on ruining my concentration by yelling out every title to me at full volume, interspersed with stories about every old engine part and bottle top in his shed. I was tempted to share a story with Les about how clothes laundering and dentistry has come a long way since the depression.

My next stop was Tamworth, where the modern conveniences of a large rural city mix with the strange genetic lottery I expect you might see in the deep south of the United States. I bought some records from a local guy called Dale, who turned out to be the only Johnny Cash tribute act personally known to and endorsed by the Cash family. He looked and sounded just like Johnny, with a cigarette seasoned voice that sounded capable of creating planets. He sold me a framed piece of Johnny Cash memorabilia, signed by the 'Man In Black' himself about sixty years prior, which I was pretty chuffed with.

The following day I arrived at Moree and their famous Artesian Aquatic Centre. I soaked in the forty-degree mineral pool as I tried to avoid the leers of the seventy-five-year-old chicks. I understood of course; it's not every day a young forty-seven-year-old buck from down south with a three-pack rocks up to the pool!

I settled into three days of being septuagenarian eye candy, knowing full well that if one of them told me they had a big punk collection and wanted sex in exchange, they would have me over a barrel, metaphorically if not literally.

Record/Chapter 22

The Johnnys — Highlights Of A Dangerous Life
(1986)

Vinyl on the Road, Series 2: The Country Bumpkin
Hotpool Escape & Record Hunt, Episode 2

After three days of fending off indecent proposals from septuagenarians at the Moree pool and feeling like I was in a bad version of the movie 'Cocoon', I thought I'd better look for some records.

I took twenty minutes to find one place in the dark. Four millennial housemates barely averted their eyes from the television as I plucked one record of use out of 200. Thankfully it was the uber cool album *Highlights Of A Dangerous Life* by Aussie cowboy punk rockers The Johnnys. I offered them $10, but none of the millennials had change (what are the chances?), so they said just to take it. Walking down the driveway in the dark, I fist bumped the air, a small victory for generation X over hipster millennial slackers. I shouldn't be too harsh though; millennials will be paying off the Covid hoax debt for the next seventy-five years. Sorry guys.

I picked up a bunch of rare Aussie rock from a toothless old crone who was selling her ex's records out of spite. Being addicted to vinyl, her ex's feelings were the least of my concern as I began drooling over bands like Carson, Madder Lake and Buffalo. I could sense she had no idea of the value, so I could have lowballed her; but I felt sorry for her homeless looking son, who looked like he could use a lift. I offered her $500, which made the son's bloodshot eyes widen as he no doubt started calculating how many 'fifties' he'd be able to score from his local dealer with his share of the loot. I shouldn't judge though; the half a Coke bottle with some garden hose attached lying on the front steps could have just been a quirky garden ornament.

I stopped in Dubbo on the way home. I was in the mood for some James Last, so popped into one of the local charity shops. A sign on the door said 'sharp knives available on request' (I did say I was in Dubbo). To give ninety-year-old Percy behind the counter something to talk about at bingo, I asked him, "Would you have anything in a fifteen-inch Rambo combat knife? I need something in case the zombies come!" He made my week when he rang the bell for assistance and asked his eighteen-year-old assistant the exact same question, including the zombie bit. I'm more easily pleased than most humans.

Record/Chapter 23

Alice Cooper — Constrictor (1986)

Vinyl on the Road, Series 3: The Major's Creek
Folkerdose Festival, Episode 1

I arrived at Major's Creek Friday afternoon, knowing I'd found the entry to the festival when I spotted a guy in his seventies who looked like Willie Nelson had collided with a rainbow. I quickly set up my marquee and tent before sinking a few beers, which I hoped would quell my instinct to automatically roll my eyes at public servants from Canberra with stupid beards wearing Alfie caps and carrying Peruvian style man bags.

The best (and worst) customer of the day was a very disturbing looking festival volunteer in khakis who reminded me of Robert DeNiro in *Taxi Driver*. He told me he had an acquired brain injury from being attacked and was the most paranoid person I'll ever meet. I told him he hasn't met my father. He rattled on to me for ages with conspiracy theories on 9/11, JFK, the moon landing, and the CIA in the U.S. bringing most of the drugs into the country. I actually agreed with him on most points, but felt in danger of being bored to death (by suicide). It wasn't a complete waste of time thankfully, as, high on the spectrum or not, he did buy a shitload of vinyl, including Alice Cooper's *Constrictor* album. He wasn't to know, but the sleeve of the album depicted exactly how I was feeling at that moment. His helter-skelter eyes and *Cape Fear* vibe gave me visions of him returning to my tent to either kill me, or worse, talk to me until dawn about reptilian bloodlines or the earth being flat.

Although initially happy at my campsite being next to the coffee tent, I regretted it Saturday morning when the inevitable freaks who can't sleep past five-thirty a.m. started queuing up for their caffeine and day-old croissants. Despite being in the tent, I felt a bit odd being stark naked while giving myself a rub down with wet wipes (no showers weekend), while hippies ordered almond milk lattes not five metres from my bare bottom and Young M.C. sang 'Bust A Move' over the cafe stereo. If I had a partner, I probably would have busted a move with her for the memory (note to future Mrs S).

At one point during the day there was so much folk

music going on simultaneously I felt like I was going to folkerdose. More than once I wished upon a star that lightning would strike the performers and a hair metal band would descend from the heavens with huge Marshall amp stacks, plug in and launch into a song about loose women or dancing with the devil.

My flu took a turn for the worse in the evening (possibly karma for being overly critical of anyone in sandals who wasn't Jesus), so was forced to bed early while my earplugs did their best to drown out the sound of bongos which every rhythm deaf bozo seemed to want to play at the same time. At one stage I thought it wouldn't be so bad if *Cape Fear* guy from the day before came by and murdered me quietly.

Record/Chapter 24

Cole Porter — The Cole Porter Songbook

Vinyl on the Road, Series 3: The Major's Creek Folkerdose Festival, Episode 2

I awoke on Sunday morning groaning to the sound of old guys with ZZ Top beards murdering traditional Australian bush poetry; or worse, murdering their own. I grabbed the first of five coffees, and if I wasn't so tired and speaking in tongues, may have flirted with the barista. She was just my type: functionally loopy with a silver astronaut jacket, leopard print leggings, and a look in her eyes that was threatening and sexual in equal measure (gulp!). I added her to my thirty-year-long list of 'ones that got away'.

There were a number of activities and festival

weirdos to help pass the time. One guy dressed as a clown and ran around on giant Oscar Pistorius style legs (sans gun), unnerving me with his scary 'IT'-like grin. Another guy called Gramophone Man dressed up like Buster Keaton and DJ'd the 1930s Cole Porter catalogue through an actual gramophone attached to an ex-ice cream cart. The gramophone speaker smoked up at one point which I thought was pretty rock n' roll.

An old festival veteran who looked like Gandalf from *Lord Of The Rings* came up to me looking quite 'sleepy', asking if I knew what he was looking for. "No, sorry mate, do you know what you're looking for?" I asked.

"I'm pretty sure you know what I'm looking for," he said.

"Dude, I don't even know what I'm looking for!" I said.

Feeling an Abbot and Costello routine coming on, I walked backwards towards the coffee tent giving him the peace sign which seemed to make him happy.

I caught a 'magic' show, though I use the term magic loosely. A moustachioed guy dressed like an 1800s shopkeeper sat inside a neon lit hula hoop playing with a glass ball like it held the mysteries of the universe. I waited with bated breath for the moment when he'd make the ball float in mid-air… but nope, he just played with it more dramatically in time with the spooky music. I tried not to boo. Next was a scantily clad hula hoop dancer, who managed to get three disco lit hoops going around her waist and one on each arm at the same time. Between the light show and the lack of clothing I didn't know where to look, but was nevertheless grateful my macular degeneration hadn't fully kicked in.

Record/Chapter 25

Pink Floyd — The Division Bell (1994)

Vinyl on the Road, Series 4: The Hopping Mad Easter Tour, Episode 1

I got fed up early by people asking me if I had a certain band, me fetching out three records of said band, and no further action being taken because they didn't expect a pristine copy of an album they'll likely never see again in this or the next lifetime, to cost $40. Gits.

A guy with a sensible haircut and sandals enjoyed telling me in detail for way too long the process he uses to convert his records to digital format. I made the mistake of asking how he deals with the crackly bits. He said it can take hours and hours to get even a few songs recorded perfectly with the nerdy procedure he was referring to, and which I was involuntarily ignoring after the third minute. I imagined his wife spending those hours and hours daydreaming about smothering him in his sleep.

Suicide beckoned again a short time later when a customer engaged me in the following conversation:

Him: "You got any Pink Floyd?"
Me: "Yep, four albums, there you go," (show albums to customer, he buys none... of course).
Him: "I've got a blue vinyl of the *Division Bell* album, unopened!"
Me: "Wow!"
Him: "Yeah never played, unopened."
Me: "Wow!"
Him: "Yeah took it home when I bought it, never opened ay."
Me: "Really!"
Him: "Yeah, *Division Bell*, blue vinyl, unopened."
Me: "Did you say unopened?"
Him: "Yeah man, unopened."
Me: "Do you know where I can get killed around here?"

An old codger took issue with my balloon cowboy hat as I stood behind my vinyl crates.

"What are you wearing that for?" he asked.

"The kids like it," I said.

"Won't do your sales any good, you look ridiculous," he stated with the brutal honesty of the soon to be departed.

"Well, thank you for your opinion, sir," I replied. I wanted to add, "Now if you'll kindly fuck off and die," or at least knock out one of his two remaining teeth. But tact and good manners got the better of me. Besides, I couldn't remember when I had my last tetanus shot.

Record/Chapter 26

Tom Waits — Blue Valentine (1978)

Vinyl on the Road, Series 4: The Hopping Mad Easter Tour, Episode 2

First customer of the day was a late fifties bogan guy with a grey flowing mullet, who spent twenty minutes regaling me with the highlights of his gig-going career. The only thing that stopped me nodding off into my thick shake was when he told me his name was Panther. Seriously. I was tempted to say, 'Wow, my name is Hawk', knowing he'd take me completely seriously.

Yummy mummies eyed off my short shorts and youthful brown stallion-like legs (steady dear reader), but I think any passing lust may have been mitigated by my balloon cowboy hat, which caused eyes to glaze over in confusion and at least one shopping trolley to run into a support pole.

I spotted a very tall solidly built twenty-five-year-old woman looking at my records. It turned out she was a he, a lovely natured guy, six feet four inches tall, in a dress, a black bob wig and size fifteen flats. Steve/Stephanie and I had a good old chat about Tom Waits' album *Blue Valentine*. I feared for the journey and challenges he faced, with no obvious female hormones present and being built like a second rower and blessed with hands that could punch a coconut open. I'm not particularly religious, but I said a silent prayer for him, and hoped he'd be able to look after himself should morons trouble him (or her).

There was a panicked rush to the supermarket as every bogan and his dog stocked up on enough beer and food to get them through a whole day with nothing open. This generally required two to three trolleys with 70% beer slabs, 20% soft drink, and a few cursory food items; usually a combination of processed meat, a few loaves of white bread, and the odd box of sugary cereal. I played a game where I tried to spot three healthy items in the one trolley. The closest I got was some grapes and choc coated muesli bars.

Back to my Airbnb accommodation, where I practised making balloon Easter bunnies, being fairly confident I was the only forty-seven-year-old in the world doing so, while trying to convince myself of my renaissance man-ness.

Record/Chapter 27

INXS — Shabooh Shoobah (1982)

Vinyl on the Road, Series 4: The Hopping Mad Easter Tour, Episode 3

I arrived early at the shopping centre on Easter Saturday, hoping to beat the masses for a park close to the entry to unload. I didn't realise the sweaty masses were instigating the second part of their Easter shopping contingency plan; i.e. turn up as early as possible to: a) make sure the supermarket is 'definitely' open and that the powers that be weren't planning on pulling some crazy two days closed in a row shit. And b) pick up the beer slabs they couldn't fit in the Hyundai on Thursday, just in case they run out. Only a theory.

A large middle-aged nerdy Greek looking lady,

maybe sixty, was gushing over INXS's album *Shabooh Shoobah* and told me she had something akin to a Michael Hutchence shrine in her bedroom, including posters on her ceiling. The long winter evenings must fly by, I thought, and said a silent prayer that she'd find the courage to move out of home before she retires.

Had a close call when a couple of likely lads wandered over to my stall. They looked sixty going on eighty due to a lifetime of sun, smokes and piss. They started manhandling my Neil Young collection in a manner that caused my Bernard Black-like bristles to… well… bristle. Thankfully the records were replaced undamaged, save for a little loss to the sleeve sheen due to midday bourbon breath.

A guy called Bob, also of the sixty going on eighty variety, complete with a gorgeous half Filipino baby (must have been love), got my hopes up when he mentioned he had a stack of 80's punk and a few thousand other records at home. I said I'd sleep with him if I could have a look. Not really, but from the description of the records, I'd definitely have considered first base if it came to it.[1]

---

[1] *Disclaimer: I mean 1980's first base, not 2023 first base. Either way, I'm scared of the lengths I would go to for vinyl.*

Record/Chapter 28

Slim Whitman — I'll Never Stop Loving You
(1961)

Vinyl on the Road, Series 5: The Flapping Mad
Riverina Tour

I ran a stall in the dead of Winter in Leeton, NSW as part of their first ever Art Deco Festival. I wasn't sure how my Iron Maiden records went with the theme but was nevertheless grateful to be able to make a few bucks and eye off some country flappers (for the instantly offended, a: I don't care. And b: see context below).

Around lunchtime I felt a severe tightness in my chest and thought this could be 'it'. I prayed that it wasn't, as if given the choice, I clearly wouldn't have opted to die standing in the teeth chattering cold in

Leeton while a toothless old crone regaled me with her love of Slim Whitman's *I'll Never Stop Loving You*. But I soon realised it was just hypothermia setting in. My organs continued to cramp until two p.m. when the organisers sensibly called time.

Back to the hotel to make myself beautiful for the Flappers and Felons Ball. In the evening I made my way into Leeton's beautiful Roxy theatre, stopping for a photo out the front with the promo flapper showgirls. I asked them what they were doing after the show. Their raised eyebrows and lips left little doubt the answer was 'not you'. I was seated at a table with a farmer called Chris (about seventy), and his wife (about forty), a cute little thing whose bogan Aussie accent cut through the music like a bandsaw.

There were plenty of 1930's style dancing girls in short skirts and feathers, intermittently spoiled by a four-man singing group who made the Delltones look sprightly. A sexy girl in a white flapper dress and pearls made all the boys tongues drop to the floor with a rendition of... I can't remember, I wasn't paying attention. The partners of the men at the tables elbowed their fellas to remind them they were there. The photographer came by and said, "Amazing isn't she, and only 15!" I tried not to feel too guilty as my boy brain proceeded to short circuit and fizz. In my defence, I left my glasses at home.[2]

---

[2] *If you identify as a 1930's flapper, i.e. sassy, stylish, brash, daring and sexy... ahem... message me immediately.*

Record/Chapter 29

The Hard Ons — Love Is A Battlefield Of Wounded Hearts (1989)

Vinyl on the Road, Series 6: The 'Why Do I Do This?' Batemans Bay/Ulladulla Summer Tour, Episode 1

Grabbed my morning coffee at the most hipster cafe in town, complete with cable spool tables, beards, and products on offer such as quinoa, turmeric juice and cacao nibs.

Just after setting up my stall, an old rough-looking moustachioed security guard came over and introduced himself as Jimi Hendrix. Being a smart arse, I instantly replied.

"Nice to meet you Jimi, I'm Gene, Gene Simmons." He didn't bat an eyelid as he pulled out his business card: 'Jimi Hendricks'. I asked him what pisses him off more, people making fun of his name, or people telling him he must get sick of people making fun of his name. The dead pan look through his yellowed chain smoker eyes was enough to make me instantly change the subject.

I met the owner of Utopia Records in Sydney. We talked for ages about music, vinyl obsession and the Hard Ons' brilliant album *Love Is A Battlefield Of Wounded Hearts*, before he relieved me of $400 worth of records. Wallet bulging profusely, I made a mental note to order the prawn version of whatever I saw on a dinner menu that evening (when you're fifty and single, it's the small things).

A lovely lady in her sixties called Diane told me she had a record shop in Milton thirty-six years ago and had tons of vinyl at home buried somewhere. After spitting my coffee over her blouse, I managed to get her number and told her I'd have her babies if she'd let me have a look… not really, but she could tell by my excited girly voice that I probably would have, biological miracles notwithstanding. I decided if she propositioned me and had at least twenty-five promo records, I was all in.

Lots of mouth breathers looking at my records; the ones where you say hello right to their face as they're browsing and get nothing back, or maybe a grunt. I always have visions of firing a rubber band into their foreheads or throwing water in their faces. I'm worried that one day pretty soon I might actually start doing it.

After finishing up for the day, I went to see the record collection of a couple in their seventies. Bob and Pam lived in a *Deliverance* style retirement village, complete with eerie ponds, ugly cabins and residents who probably weren't captured in the last (or any) census. I felt I was constantly being watched, probably by someone within easy reach of a chainsaw who hadn't seen the outside world since Woodstock. Bob drove me in from the gate in case I got 'lost'. Feeling uneasy, I did a cursory check for a weapon before offering them a borderline insulting price for their unplayed copy of the Beatles debut album, *Please Please Me*. A sigh of relief when they seemed happy with my offer, though I still had my doubts about Bob. When Pam mentioned she had 6,000 DVD's and asked if I knew where she could find some more, Bob gave her a 'one of these days Alice' look that told me if his buttons were pushed too far, not even his dodgy hip or walking cane would save you.

Record/Chapter 30

Motorhead — Rock 'n' Roll (1987)

Vinyl on the Road, Series 6: The Why Do I Do This Summer Tour, Episode 2

I had a Frank Spencer-esque start to the day when I turned into the main street of Milton and one of my balloon boxes decided to exit the front passenger window which I'd conveniently left open. I experienced one of those moments when you feel like you're outside of your body watching the absurdity of your life in action; in this case a forty-seven-year-old dashing in between passing trucks to pick up stray balloons and flyers with the help of a passing lawn mower guy which somehow made it worse.

A day of painful customers, including a guy in his

sixties who was three cans short of a six pack: most likely from living at home with his mum for sixty years rather than from genuine mental illness. He spent an hour explaining the process of how he converted his Beatles collection into digital format. I'm sure if I wandered off to the gents he would have kept talking until I came back; I don't think he cared if anyone was listening. By the time he left I was wishing the Beatles were drowned at birth.

A pair of girls who could have passed for Kath and Kim, complete with the boganest of accents and Wagga Wagga DNA, tested the limits of acceptable human endurance by talking endlessly about every band they had a mild interest in, including a fuzzy account of the infamous Queanbeyan leg of Motorhead's world tour on the back of their album *Rock 'n' Roll*. At that point, after a solid ninety minutes at my stall with no vinyl purchased, I couldn't decide who I'd rather have smothered with a pillow, them or me. In hindsight, I think either would have made me happy.

After packing up, I went to look at the collection of an old chain-smoking wreck of a guy called Kevin out at Dolphin Point. Kev's eyes were so damaged they were almost beautiful; sort of like someone took the yellowish irises of a cat and shattered them into a thousand pieces. He was a bachelor and complained of feeling lonely.

"You're preaching to the converted mate," I said. "Have you thought of getting a dog?" I briefly entertained the idea of doing him up an internet dating profile but thought I'd pushed enough shit uphill for one day/lifetime.

I arrived back at the hostel, hoping my summer stint at the Bay would go quickly. A week might be a long time in politics, but it's an eternity in mullet central.

Record/Chapter 31

Jimmy Barnes — Freight Train Heart (1987)

Vinyl on the Road, Series 6: The Why Do I Do This Summer Tour, Episode 3

I had breakfast at one of the fancier cafes in the Bay. It occurred to me that those annoying hipsters could be rubbing off on me. Not only did I spend $20 on eggs on toast, but I was also more disappointed than I should have been that my avocado didn't arrive smashed.

I was being a bit flirty with a girl at my stall after I told her she looked a bit like Amy Winehouse and her eyelids nearly batted off. Things got a bit heated when she started telling me about her partying days in Berlin.

"Does that mean you're a bad girl?" I asked.

"Maybe," she said, winking at me. I told her she'd

be in all sorts of trouble if I was twenty years younger. She then turned to the lady three crates down who heard the whole conversation and said, "So Mum, are you buying anything?" Yep, just like Ralph Malph, I still got it.

Another customer was possibly Jimmy Barnes' biggest fan. After buying his album *Freight Train Heart* (fun fact: produced and partly written and performed by members of Journey), she told me she had a huge tattoo of Barnesy's mug on her back, and judging from her limbs, a collection of other nightmarish ink circa 1978. She wasn't entirely horrible looking, but considering the Barnesy obsession, she would have likely been surprised that, in a hypothetical scenario, I would have slept with Lizzy Birdsworth from *Prisoner Cell Block H* before she'd get a look in.

A guy who looked in his fifties but more likely in his twenties (decomposing skin on the living never a good look), asked me if I had any Dead Kennedys.

"Why, you're not going to buy any even if I did!" I tried not to say out loud. He left quickly, but not before I had an 'Aha' moment… that's what crystal meth smells like!

I arrived back at the hostel to find someone had stuck a piece of chewing gum to my undies hanging on the clothesline. Nothing much shocks me anymore, I just put it down to my suffering quota not being reached for that week.

Record/Chapter 32

Metallica — Creeping Death (1984)

Vinyl on the Road, Series 6: The Why Do I Do This Summer Tour, Episode 4

I woke in the early hours after a dream in which I was in a sexual relationship with a hippy girl who was completely loopy. Just as in the case if this was my current reality, I found it both disturbing and awesome in equal measure. To get back to sleep I did a few rounds of 'Wim Hof' breathing and awoke refreshed and ready for whatever sun affected oddballs the day had in store.

I had a brief scare when Rain Man with the Beatles obsession from two days ago appeared without warning before me and started recommending the best way to clean vinyl: something about a stool, a damp cloth and some highly flammable liquid. I was about to settle in for another hour of 'uh-huh', 'is that right?' and 'really!', when he took off without warning. My sigh of relief could have blown out a hundred candles.

A woman from Nowra messaged me asking if I'd be interested in buying six identical Metallica *Creeping Death* picture discs, which she said she acquired when she swapped them for a bird; so not weird or suspicious at all. I suspected the records could be hot property, but I'd be mostly selling them to the poor, so I figured it would sort of even out.

I had to grin and bear it as an older mentally ill guy who drooled like a Saint Bernard slobbered all over my discount crates. The Captain and Tenille didn't seem to mind.

Plenty of animal balloon work in between record sales. Yummy mummies stood spellbound as they watched me make a two-tone horse with a mane and bridle out of balloons in three minutes flat; no doubt (in my imagination at least) wondering what other miracles a humble and majestically handsome record dealer could perform with his hands. I could have told them I also know Kung Fu, never forget to take out the trash, and often vacuum in my underwear, but didn't want anyone to feint from swooning. Yes ladies, I'm nothing if not considerate.

Back to a 'bogans by the sea' club for dinner. Kids with mullets to the left of me and hipsters with lumberjack beards to the right, I let out a huge grumpy sigh, praying that this was all a bad dream and I would wake up somewhere in the vicinity of 1982, preferably at a Divinyls gig.

Record/Chapter 33

Rose Tattoo — Assault And Battery (1981)

Vinyl on the Road, Series 6: The Why Do I Do This Summer Tour, Episode 5

I woke up in the early hours after a bad dream in which I was forty-seven and all alone in a dodgy cabin on a windy rainy night, panicking that my only significant skill outside record dealing and writing is making horses with manes and bridles out of balloons. I breathed a sigh of relief as my life isn't nearly that tragic (citations pending).

A seasoned trolley collector called Ron, whose IQ seemed to match his age (about fifty-eight), bought Rose Tattoo's 'Assault And Battery'. I was then on tenterhooks (not), as he related the story of how he acquired his current Ned Kelly ring. Apparently he tried it on when visiting a bikie clubhouse. He couldn't get it off, so was given an ultimatum of either handing over $500 for the ring or having his finger removed by the sergeant at arms. Lovely.

On the way home I stopped off at Nowra to pick up the Metallica albums from the lady who had swapped a bird for them (see last episode). Hands down the weirdest pick up I've ever had. The house was like something out of a horror movie, including wrought iron gates and windows like eyes, with parts of mannequins and stained mattresses in the yard. The lady came out to the padlocked iron gates and passed the records through for me to inspect.

"So," I said, "You took all these Metallica albums in exchange for a bird?"

"Yes," she replied, completely deadpan.

"I have to admit when you said that it sounded a little strange!" I exclaimed.

"Not really," she replied in a monotone. I wanted to probe for more details of possibly the weirdest transaction involving vinyl ever in the history of the world, but her Norman Bates type blank look told me she was done. Plus, I had a feeling someone was aiming a bow and arrow at me from inside the house, and I really didn't want it to end in remote north Nowra... not when there was still a chance I could get laid again before retirement.

Record/Chapter 34

Billy Joel — Turnstiles (1976)

A Career Wake Up Call

My dog Charlie gave me the look of death as I left him on the veranda in the rain and cold. I hope he'll forgive me when we meet in heaven (or some other universe), where I'd like to think dogs will be able to talk about records and play board games.

After several years out of the public service, I arrived in Canberra for an interview with my old employer, not entirely sure whether I was ready to sit behind a desk again and sacrifice a life of record hunting, surfing, spending almost every waking moment with Charlie and hobo-ing around the country.

I was led to a waiting room by an ex-colleague who was on the selection panel. It happened to be a carer's room with a bunch of toys. In an ideal world I would have loved to have picked a teddy bear out of the box and held him during the interview for comfort (note to the woke: all teddy bears are 'him' unless they have a bow in their hair and long eyelashes, irrespective of missing genitalia. I know it's messed up, but it just is). My ex-colleague wouldn't have minded, but he couldn't vouch for the other panel members or how it would affect my chances. He said if I could find him a copy of Billy Joel's *Turnstiles,* he'd see what he could do with the selection report. He obviously didn't realise as a record dealer I could throw a dart at my mountain of records and hit three copies of the album with the same dart.

During the interview I wondered whether it was obvious I paid $2 for my Italian wool suit at the Moss Vale rubbish tip recycling centre. The suit must have looked reasonably hot, judging by the sexy middle aged blonde woman who half tripped over when she spotted me. It could have been a crack in the pavement, but at that point I needed all the confidence I could get, so I stuck to my theory.

I didn't end up getting the job, which was probably a good thing: a) I couldn't (and still can't) reconcile loving a dog as much as I love Charlie and working nine to five. And b) I found a record collection two weeks later that netted me over $30K in six weeks. Baddabing!

Record/Chapter 35

Mad Max — Original Movie Soundtrack (1980)

My Obsession With An Oz Cinema Masterpiece

Mad *Max* has ranked in my top five movies of all time since the age of twelve. Of course, at that age, I didn't know what to make of the crazy dialogue, the dystopian vision of the future, or the outright weirdness of the bad guys. But with hot cars and bikes, guns, leather and lawlessness, there wasn't much not to like.

I came close to buying a replica of Max's black 'Interceptor' vehicle in 2014 after taking a redundancy from the public service. There were (bizarrely) two beautiful examples for sale at that time. If my pay out was a little bigger, I would have made possibly the most foolish purchase of my life. On the one hand, I knew I could have tripled my money pretty easily. But I also knew if I went through with it, I would never sell it, and likely ask someone to put me in it when I die, set it on fire and roll it off a cliff in true *Mad Max* fashion... seriously.

I loved Steve Bisley's character the 'Goose'. His carefree attitude, cheeky sense of humour and swagger resonated strongly with me, and still does to this day. In the last few years, I read his two autobiographies, *Stillways* and *All The Burning Bridges*. I instinctively knew Steve was essentially playing himself in the movie even before reading them.

Stillways is possibly the most beautiful autobiography I've ever read, portraying both the beautiful innocence and sheer cruelty he experienced as a child. Being a dog lover, one passage I found particularly moving. Steven returns to the family farm after a few weeks visiting relatives, away from his abusive father. He's sitting in a paddock repeatedly trying to get his dog Duke to round up the cows. Duke can't be bothered and just comes up and nuzzles into Steven's neck, both boy and dog comforted by the feeling of finally being home. Makes me a bit teary even writing that; not very 'Goose' like of me I must say. Still, I'm sure Mr Bisley would understand.

Perhaps it's a law of attraction thing but being such a *Mad Max* fanatic has led me to random meetings with several people involved, at least by association, with its filming.

One work colleague's mother once lived in the house Max and Jessie live in in the first movie.

A friend of mine Madge, one of the grooviest women of her age I know, used to date the brother of director George Miller. I couldn't have been more jealous hearing stories of actresses turning up naked at the door, and opening the freezer one day to find a bunch of dead crows.

A few years ago, a customer of mine told me the story of how his dad, a truck driver, was randomly asked to drive some gear around the set of *Mad Max 2*. Being impressed with his driving skills, the producers asked if he'd do the final stunt of the movie, where Max's truck runs off the road and flips over. "Sure mate, just tell me where to aim it," he said, being the epitome of the easy-going Oz bloke. The story goes he hit the target perfectly, and the rest is history.

Another friend Kate knows the guy responsible for the vehicle behemoths in *Mad Max: Fury Road*. And a few years ago, I played poker against disabled actor Quentin Kenihan, who played Corpus Colossus in that movie. Among the many talents he had was taking $500 from me in one of the sickest poker bluffs ever seen at Crown Casino (R.I.P. buddy). And finally, through a contact in the film industry, I obtained one of the few original scripts of *Mad Max 2*.

Although admittedly a little tragic, I haven't lost hope of owning my own 'Interceptor' one day. I may be fifty, but I can't imagine more fun than rocking up to a Macca's drive thru in it, dressed head to toe in leathers with my very own blue heeler riding shotgun. I've said it before and I'll say it again… one at a time ladies!

Record/Chapter 36

The Celibate Rifles — Dancing Barefoot (1988)

Brushes With Fame, Episode 1

The first celebrity I remember seeing in real life was in 1985 at a Gold Coast theme park, where I queued up for the waterslides behind Bevan from *Young Talent Time*. Thirteen-year-old me wished upon a star that Danni (Minogue) or Tina (Arena) would turn up shortly in pert bikinis, just gagging to talk to an olive-skinned bean pole with buck teeth whose interests included Dungeons and Dragons and becoming world champion at Galaga.

In 2000 a friend of a friend invited me to dinner with her brother, British Hollywood actor Ben Chaplin. You may remember him from *The Truth About Cats*

And Dogs with Uma Thurman. A hilarious guy, he recounted the filming of *Birthday Girl* with Nicole Kidman. She's a lousy kisser apparently, which didn't really surprise me, as by that stage she was already on the way to having a face like the surface of a refrigerator, which surely must make getting purchase a bit of a challenge. A fun night, though as I was broke, having just taken a year off to study, it was a tad demoralising watching Ben pull out fistsful of hundred dollar notes to pay for dinner for twenty-five.

A few years ago, I met ex-Celibate Rifles bass player Rudy Morabito when he wandered into my shop. We both got a kick out of realising he played on the *Dancing Barefoot* EP which was sitting in my crates. He told me about the time they supported the Ramones at CBGB's in New York. Apparently, Joey was quite clumsy and would be falling all over the stairs even sober. Joey told Rudy he loved his bass playing and asked if he wanted to come out for a night on the town. Unbelievably Rudy said he was tired and wanted to get an early night. Yes, you read that right; he turned down a night out with *Joey fucking Ramone*! If I went out for a night on the town with Joey Ramone thirty-three years ago, it would have come up in every second conversation I had with someone up until now, no matter the context. I 'am' a bit special though.

Record/Chapter 37

Coldplay — Viva La Vida (2008)

Brushes With Fame, Episode 2

Tim Rogers from You Am I wandered in for a browse one day. We introduced ourselves: him to a nobody record dealer with a side-line in animal balloons, me to an Oz indie rock legend who I've air guitared to in my living room to more times than I can count. He wasn't to know I'd probably obtained him a few more record sales from bludgeoning my fellow tourists over the head with my You Am I mix tape on a week-long tour of Ireland in 1997.

Rob Younger from Radio Birdman has wandered into my shop a few times. The first couple of times I was a bit awestruck, much like Garth and Wayne with Alice

Cooper in *Wayne's World*; the difference being I didn't even feel worthy enough to let him know I'm not worthy. Finally, with a voice which I thought had broken in 1987, I simply said.

"You're Rob aren't you?" His immediate rolling of the eyes let me know that I was indeed not worthy, as he said (or may as well have).

"Yes, I'm Rob Younger, godfather of Australian punk and indie rock, give me whatever the hell it is you want me to sign you unworthy cretin and I'll be on my way." He was pretty cool actually.

The last brush with fame was actually my late brother Craig's. I had been to see Coldplay with my ex in 2009. I later found out that late that evening Craig was at Sydney casino, drunkenly chatting to and getting on like a house on fire with some British guy for two hours. Eventually the guy says to Craig.

"You don't know who I am do you?"

"Nah mate, no idea," says Craig. Once the cat was out of the bag, Craig told Chris Martin his childhood must have been shit, what with being forced to sit down at a piano for most of it. Chris agreed with Craig that it was indeed shit. They got on so well, Chris Martin offered my brother a 200k job and asked him to come on tour with him. Unfortunately, Craig wasn't in a position to take up the offer, as he'd only recently had his arm torn almost completely off in a horrific workplace accident. As my brother recounted his encounter with Chris, we both dwelled on the random and precarious nature of life; how being at the right place at the right (or wrong) time, can change your life in an instant.

Record/Chapter 38

Front End Loader — Last Of The V8 Interceptors (1997)

Memorable Gigs, Episode 1

In 1996 I saw Suicidal Tendencies play at Newcastle University, supported by my old school mate Phil's Newcastle band 'The Wash' (more on Phil later). You would have needed a jackhammer to get the smile off my face as Robert Trujillo (before going soft and joining Metallica) slapped the shit out of his bass three metres from my naked eyes, and Rocky George nearly brought me to orgasm with his guitar solo on 'You Can't Bring Me Down'; possibly the sickest thirty seconds of live music I've ever witnessed.

Another great gig was in 2000 when I saw my

cousin David's indie/hard rock band Cheezcake play to a dozen people at a Newcastle pub. Despite the truly awful band name, their music was bloody awesome, in the vein of Rage Against The Machine. David was/is a ridiculously talented drummer, and cousin of Chrissie Amphlett of The Divinyls. He studied in the U.S. under Billy Martin (of Iggy Pop and Medeski Martin & Wood fame) and these days keeps time for funky Gold Coast 8-piece Roots group Heavy Wax.

In my early twenties, when virtually every Sydney pub still had bands (sigh), a mate and I developed a strange addiction to seeing thrash rockers Front End Loader. They played a mix of horrible and horribly awesome songs that made you feel like they were angry at you for daring to turn up. Let's just say if you had a girl you wanted to impress, you didn't take her to a Front End Loader gig... unless she was a bad girl; but I couldn't find one of those to save myself (still can't... sigh).

Front End Loader scored big time brownie points with me when they released their 1997 album *Last Of The V8 Interceptors*. The album title being a clear reference to *Mad Max*, they included a replica yellow Pursuit Special vehicle in the film clip for the song 'Summer Hits'. When most guys my age were getting serious about careers and finding someone to make babies with, I spent my weekends at Front End Loader gigs at various Sydney pubs, losing my hearing by standing as close to the speakers as possible, singing along with gusto to songs like 'All Star Jam' and 'Four Star Heritage Arsehole'. It was only years later that I would mature into the wise cracking, humble, tragically single, majestically handsome, record dealing and animal balloon making renaissance man you see before you today.

Record/Chapter 39

Ramones — Brain Drain (1989)

Memorable Gigs, Episode 2

In 1994, in an exercise of extreme pleasure and pain, I saw the Ramones play at the second Big Day Out concert in Sydney. Being a rabid Ramones fan (who to this day would be sporting a Johnny Ramone haircut if genetics would just cooperate), the splitting headache I had on the day didn't stop me getting to the front of the mosh pit and 'Gabba Gabba Hey'ing' at the top of my lungs. I would regularly take the Ramones album *Brain Drain* to parties, ruining the vibe by putting on something like 'Don't Bust My Chops' or 'Pet Sematary', standing guard at the stereo in case anyone dared switch it off. Of course, I eventually stopped such childish behaviour; around age forty-two if memory serves.

In 2012 in Las Vegas, I saw ZZ Top play at the House Of Blues. Standing directly below Billy Gibbons, I experienced another orgasmic musical moment when Billy looked straight at me with his two-foot beard, furry guitar and expensive teeth, blowing my top (ZZ Top's words not mine) with an extended solo on 'I Need You Tonight'. This is by far the song I've air guitared to most in my life, and like a Pavlovian dog, will automatically start air guitaring to it if I randomly hear it while I'm out and about, no matter where I am (fair warning and apologies in advance to future Mrs S).

In 2014 I finally got to see the Baby Animals on the back of their album *This Is Not The End*. I've been in love with Suzi DeMarchi since 1990, so naturally had yet another orgasmic moment watching her rock out in the… ahem… flesh. Her husky alpha female voice does things to me that tact prevents me from putting into words. Needless to say, I felt like a cigarette making my way home from the ANU bar.

Despite being a devastatingly eligible bachelor, if anyone knows of a good therapist who can help with any of the abovementioned *Mondo Bizarro* psychological issues (see what I did there?), please feel free to get in touch.

Record/Chapter 40

Bob Marley And The Wailers — Confrontation
(1983)

The Old Man and The Sea

I can't say I was a natural water baby. One of my earliest memories is going for swimming lessons as a six-year-old, slowly motoring our way down to Lake Macquarie on a red double decker school bus in 1978. My stomach flip-flopped at the thought of the black bottomless monster-filled water and agonising death that surely awaited me. I managed, through tears, to float on my back and perform a panic-stricken dog paddle, with my teacher Mrs Jarvie's comforting hand for support; but only managed to smile again once we were all dried off and back in our uniforms, standing side by side at the boys' urinal and sword fighting with our pee.

In 2008, during my year living and working in the Solomon Islands, I often spent weekends with a bunch of friends, hiring a local with a banana boat to take us out to one of the islands. We were returning from Tulagi one weekend (a two-hour trip from Honiara), when halfway home we ran out of fuel. The 'captain' had spare fuel but the motor wouldn't restart. As we listened to 'Buffalo Soldier' on the captain's 1984 ghetto blaster, a storm then naturally descended on our piss-weak boat, complete with sideways rain and 200-foot-high water funnels (the law of attraction doesn't work for Blackadder type cynics like me; *The Secret* my arse). Someone pulled out a satellite phone and called for help as we bailed out water with our hats and Bob Marley's voice cracked up under speakers clearly not designed for a monsoon. I had visions of us huddled in a circle in our life jackets, waiting for the inevitable great white to bite us in half as we shared the captain's last soggy joint. Finally, with MacGyver-like ingenuity, the captain sucked fuel through a hose and got the engine going. We then endured an hour of being pounded by six-foot waves before reaching the shore. I couldn't walk properly for a week, but thankfully there was no lasting damage to my pride... or perfectly formed bottom.

Record/Chapter 41

Joe Dolce — Shaddap You Face (1981)

Rad Fads and Wish I Hads, Episode 1

As a nine-year-old, records and record players were just a fad. I thought my school friend Bradley was the shit with his toy turntable, whose crap speakers we would crank up to full, pissing off the neighbours with Joe Dolce's 'Shaddap You Face' which made us nearly wet ourselves with delight, no matter how many times we heard it. Having never grown up, at fifty, the same thing happens to me today when I watch the fart scene in *Blazing Saddles*.

1981 was a huge year for fads. I spent most of the year pining for a deluxe Coca Cola or Fanta yo-yo. I was perpetually frustrated that, despite a good throwing arm,

I didn't have the dexterity to pull off a 'rock the cradle' or 'Eifel Tower' move, and would often smack myself in the head trying to do loop de loops. The Coca Cola Yo-Yo Team visited our school one day. Somehow, they got to wear team Coca Cola tracksuits and play with yo-yo's all day instead of going to school. I hated them.

The highlight of my week was going to Broadmeadow roller rink on Saturday afternoons. If you're a millennial reading this, OMFG you missed out big time! Roller skating rinks in the early 80s were the most fun you could ever have on eight wheels. In a time before smartphones, when screen time was limited to your rich friend with an Atari after school (thanks Nige), the roller rink had it all: tough guys, hot chicks, speed, collisions, loud new wave music, creepy DJ's, and childhood peacocking. One corner of the rink went up into a ramp, where mulleted old guys (fifteen) would do crazy jumps in their speed skates and shiny jackets, impressing girls called Debbie with white skates and perms. Ten-year-old me sat on the Frogger machine in the corner with a fake earring and smoking lolly 'Fags', looking aloof and waiting for a gorgeous girl with speed skates, cherry red lipstick and a top-of-the-line yo-yo to walk up and ask me to marry her. Still wouldn't mind…

Record/Chapter 42

Simply Red — Stars (1991)

Rad Fads and Wish I Hads, Episode 2

Being a vain thirteen-year-old, and wanting to stand out from the other nerds, I had to do something about my hair. After seeing a cool band photo (probably Ultravox), I raced up to the hairdresser and asked her to 'new wave' me. She layered my hair at the back in three steps and roughed up the top, making me look like Annie Lennox's snotty nosed kid brother. Mum, on seeing my noggin, took me back to the hairdresser by the elbow, demanding she fix this abomination immediately. I would eventually realise that whatever I wore or however I looked, if I didn't appear to have walked out of a Country Road catalogue, Mum was never going to be happy. We managed to agree to disagree around age forty-five.

At age twenty, being sick of having a fine, limp mop top, Mum suggested I get a body wave. I took Simply Red's *Stars* album into the hairdresser.

"Make me like Mick the ginger only shorter, and more wavy than curly," I said. I don't know whether she forgot to take the curlers out early, or kept looking at Hucknall for reference, but when the big reveal came, I couldn't close my mouth for a full minute. I had a full on, dare I say aggressive perm! It was that bad I could have doubled for Screech on *Saved By The Bell*. I went home in tears, knowing it would be six weeks before I could even think of going out in public, unless it was in the context of being an attraction at a circus sideshow (clown wig not required).

I did manage shoulder length hair once or twice and had the odd day when I thought I was pulling off a respectable smouldering Steve Kilbey (poor choice of words sorry). But unlike Rick Savage in Def Leppard, who manages to look more like a confused dog with every album, I finally realised that at some point you have to let go and work with what you got. In my case, a weird head, receding hairline and a few tufts that make me look like I'm in a permanent wind tunnel. Eleven words… if you want it, come and put a ring on it.

Record/Chapter 43

Breakdance — Original Movie Soundtrack (1984)

Rad Fads and Wish I Hads, Episode 3

In 1984, having been primed by 'Rock Steady Crew' videos, I saw the movie *Breakdance* and knew that to be a real man, I would need to start breaking quick smart. I took lessons from my mate Phil, who had impressed us all in music class with his 'breaking robot' demo. Our hyper gay music teacher Mr Simpson provided some lame piano accompaniment, which detracted somewhat from Phil's tough street moves. We became obsessed with breaking, and would drag pieces of cardboard to class, working on our moves before the teacher arrived.

After several weeks of 'training', a movie-like scenario played out in the Newcastle High gymnasium on the night of the school dance. Phil and I didn't make very convincing punks, but thought we were pretty tough with our fake earrings, black mascara and tennis headbands. We danced away in 'idle' to top 40 crap, waiting for the inevitable moment when the DJ would play something 'break worthy'. Sure enough, 'Freakshow On The Dance Floor' by the Bar-Kays started playing. But before we could bust our moves, some new kid who we hadn't seen before, dressed in a shiny red and white Marlboro jacket, started spinning around and threw down the gauntlet by pulling off a rotating turtle move that caused the kids to make a circle and see what else he had in store.

Well, Phil and I couldn't take this lying down. I also knew it was the perfect moment to prove my manhood to Tracey Hinze, who had seen me crying in the cinema at *E.T.* and asked if I was OK.

We made our way to the middle of the floor, starting with a choreographed 'breaking robot'. We then went to opposite sides of the circle and 'wormed' our way back to the centre, colliding with each other before springing up to our feet. I busted out my 'helicopter' while Phil pulled off the holy grail of breaking, the 'head spin'. As that was about all we had, we high fived and moonwalked back into the crowd, as Marlboro guy stood with his arms crossed and Tracey smiled at us, in admiration or pity I'm still not sure.

Record/Chapter 44

Van Halen — 1984 (1983)

(Less Than) Stellar Performances

In year eleven, five friends and I dressed up as The Village People and performed *In The Navy* at the school disco. Much pant-wetting laughter ensued, most notably at the 135-pound biker (yours truly) with the not terribly adhesive handlebar moustache. We were on a high having just seen the real Village People live. Only one of our group was gay, but we could all appreciate how their awesome dance moves — indeed their Milkshake — would bring all the boys to the yard.

In 2012 I braved a few stand-up comedy gigs. My best bit was a proposal for a tv show to replace *Farmer Wants A Wife*. I posited that that show was a yawn fest because young Billy in the moleskins with the sheep farm would simply choose the vacuous blonde with the big boobs, no matter how lovely or intelligent the other girls were. I thought (and still think) a much better show would be *Bikie Gang Member Wants A Wife*. I figured there could be a triathlon, including a (pole) dance-off, nude wrestling in piles of laundered cash, and loading and firing a twelve-gauge shotgun from a Harley in a bikini. I mean who wouldn't watch that shit?

In 2009 I was a finalist at the Australian Air Guitar Championships; yes, you read that right. My stage persona was 'Rocks With Wolves'. My huge foxy mullet and Ted Nugent raccoon tail made jaws drop and (in my mind at least) caused females to unconsciously bite their bottom lip. I convinced my poor ex to be my 'roadie', introducing her to the crowd as a lovely old-fashioned girl who could suck a watermelon through a straw. Although my acrobatic performance of Van Halen's 'Hot For Teacher' got a huge cheer, reigning champion 'Clay Bangers' took the title and jetted off to Finland for the world championships. I thought I had him on technical ability, but I think his Evel Knieval jumpsuit might have been the deciding factor, fashion obviously taking precedence over talent; much like an Instagram influencer. Pfffftt...

Record/Chapter 45

Wilson Phillips — Wilson Phillips (1990)

A Hopeless Hopeless Romantic, Episode 1

At year six camp I had three girls who all wanted to 'go out' with me, a feat I've never been able to repeat. At age 11, in my mind this meant holding hands a hell of a lot. I had to decide between Jodie, Sheree and Charmaine. A messenger was sent to my tent to get important inside information from me, namely: who would I kiss, and more importantly, who would I pash! Unlike modern day eleven-year-old boys who are (sadly) already familiar with every extreme of human sexuality, kissing seemed very embarrassing to me, so no I said, that would be out. As far as pashing goes, I had no bloody idea what a pash was, but it sounded kind of painful, so that would 'definitely' be out! When Friday came, I chose Charmaine as she had the cutest smile of the three candidates. We held hands and smoked hollow sticks around the campfire, as Jodie and Sheree looked on nursing their broken little hearts.

My first 'proper' girlfriend was Jo; a lovely old-fashioned girl with wholesome morals and a killer bod. I was the lowly stock boy at Grace Bros department store; she was the ladies underwear sales assistant who smiled at me whenever I dropped off a bunch of panties (I love that word). I blushed so hard I looked sunburnt, as I asked her if she needed any help unpacking the panties, sorting the panties or pricing the panties. We became an item at the work Xmas party. Sitting at a table with her and my workmates, I painfully agreed with her that the song playing, 'Hold On' by Wilson Phillips was tops. My mates, on cue, then all got up from the table, making it obvious they wanted to see us get together. And we did for a few weeks, before I dumped her. I hadn't realised her dad, Bob, worked in the electrical appliances section. He was a mean looking son of a bitch with an Elvis quiff who sneered at me every time I walked past, as if all I could think about was touching his daughter's breasts. It was of course. But at nineteen, I was too young for uphill battles (now I'm too old for them). Plus, she hadn't discovered the art of leg shaving. Otherwise, we probably would have made beautiful babies together. Sorry, Jo.

Record/Chapter 46

Warrant — Cherry Pie (1990)

A Hopeless Hopeless Romantic, Episode 2

In 1993 I was 'headhunted' to manage the stock room at Portmans ladies' fashion. A more capable twenty-one-year-old male would have slept with half of the dozen or so hot women he was surrounded by on a daily basis. Unfortunately, my shy boy genes, grungy look and textbook-worthy acne ensured another textbook entry; this time under 'how to be friend-zoned'. Every day the God of the tragically single tortured me by sending up a precession of nines and tens, rubbing it in my face by playing something on the radio like 'Cherry Pie' at the exact moment they entered the room.

I was in love with Francesca, an Italian girl hotter

than a Ferrari engine, who always seemed to be up a ladder in a tight dress and stockings, asking if I could hold her steady.

'Ummm, okay,' I would say nonchalantly, trying to simultaneously hold her calves and not feint or completely lose my poor one-track mind. I would go home and air guitar to 'Women' by Def Leppard, obsessing over Francesca and trying not to self-harm.

In 2000 I found myself in the ski fields of Slovakia. I hit it off with Adriena, an average looking hairdresser (just kidding, she was smoking hot, I was in Eastern Europe people!). After our third date, we agreed that, hypothetically at least, we would have very beautiful babies. She lost interest though one day at the ski lifts. We were queued up just ahead of a British male model called Roger, who also happened to be a stunt man and had done the jet ski work on the latest James Bond film. As Adriena's eyes glazed over at Roger's accent and biceps, I turned into Frank Spencer, jamming the pass attached to my pants in the turnstile and going arse over tit. Roger came and helped me to my feet like I weighed nothing, saying, "Easy there Tiger!", his eyes barely diverting from the swell of Adriena's breasts. The phrase 'for fucks sake' would feature, and continues to feature, predominantly in my dating life (sigh).

Record/Chapter 47

Journey — Raised On Radio (1986)

A Hopeless Hopeless Romantic, Episode 3

Astrid was a cute four-foot-eleven-inch carny who I met on Tinder and dated for a few weeks when the circus rolled into town. Constantly dressed in purple, she was a sickeningly happy soul with more piercings than I could count, who would interrupt our conversations at random moments and cartwheel down the street. Sensing my soul was more of the perpetually grumpy variety, she lit some candles, put on some relaxing music and tried to 'reiki' my glass half empty attitude back into the cosmos. I can't say that it worked, but I can say the sex was so scary it felt like I'd entered another universe. Afterwards I felt like Ben Stiller in that scene from *The Heartbreak Kid*, rocking in my chair and wondering how romance aligned with the horror filled scenes I'd just born witness to. I made a mental note to go to confession ASAP.

I worked as a bush regenerator in 1997, where I met a very cute pixie-like redhead called Claire, who came complete with freckles and an indescribably beautiful soul. The day I met her I fell head over heels in love, with a clear vision of our life together: adventures, travel, babies, laughter and love that felt like the universe was created just to accommodate it. She already had a boyfriend so I didn't voice any of that to her of course, and tried not to torture myself too much as we sat side by side in the bush near railway tracks, poisoning lantana bushes and picking ticks out of each other's hair.

A few years later, I picked up the newspaper and on the front page was a story about Claire. Working for the National Parks and Wildlife Service, she was back burning on a very still day in Sydney when the wind conditions changed unexpectedly, turning the fire on and trapping her, along with the small team she was working with. Though we had never dated and she never knew how I felt, I cried for a week at the loss of a friend who gave me a glimpse of what true love might feel like. Claire Deane, if you're reading this, in the words of my all-time favourite band, Journey, 'It Could Have Been You'. Rest in peace beautiful girl.

Record/Chapter 48

Swingers — Original Movie Soundtrack (1996)

A Hopeless Hopeless Romantic, Episode 4

Julie was a Scottish lass who frequented the Inverness bar I worked at. She always had a hot but scary posse of Scottish females in tow, each of whom could drink a 130kg rugby prop under the table. Around closing time, I would ask her how her night was going. She would respond mostly in vowels while attempting to lift my kilt. Flattered as I was, I've never been one to take advantage (unless vinyl is involved), so would walk her out to a cab and let her slap me on my kilted bottom.

'You just wait Aussie!' she would say with a wink and a hiccup. I did see her a few times... almost all of her in fact; but I had to put the brakes on after I found out she was married. I also learned that she was a known psycho hose beast, who had recently painted her hubby's BMW in a shade of hot pink and set fire to his clothes. Not the kind of empowered female I had in mind.

Mel was a regular at the bar I worked at in Brighton England. She must have been eyeing me off for several weeks, and one day found the courage to ask me out. I believe this was only the third time in human history a woman had asked a man out for a date. I was very flattered but felt a bit put on the spot, as Mel was six foot three and built like a second rower with the prettiest man hands you ever did see. I was fairly confident that in an arm wrestle scenario where she was using her bad arm and me my good one, she still would have won. Freezing and not knowing what to say, I accepted her invitation to the movies. I got through most of *Swingers* unscathed, but then during the scene where John Favreau asks Heather Graham out, she reached across and held my hand. I stared wide-eyed at the screen and silently whimpering, feeling safe in her grip but wondering how I could escape this unfortunate scenario before she invited me upstairs for coffee… and a round of arm wrestling.

Record/Chapter 49

Matt Finish — Short Note (1981)

The Great Escape

Having taken a redundancy in 2014, I spent much of the next five years hobo-ing around the country as a 'casual' vinyl record dealer; a time of deep introspection. As most guys in their forties were contending with families, careers and massive mortgages, I was surfing, practising kung fu, hanging with Charlie my dog, and wondering where the next meal or Blue Note jazz collection was coming from.

During this time, I was offered a government contract. By the end of the first week however, I had made the following 'shocking' observations:

a) most of the work people were doing largely

didn't matter: to you, to them or the people in charge (and if it did, they were either in denial, lying or utterly insane).

b) efficiency was dead in the water, primarily as everyone was on their phone half the time, either playing Pokémon Go or stalking Instagram bikini models.

c) people had found new and exciting ways to waste government money, including the creation of 'innovation' teams. In case you're not familiar, you start with a budget of say three million dollars. You then set up teams of woke gen Y's (ideally good looking and tech savvy with zero common sense), pay them more than most employees with twenty years of service, give them bean bags to work from, and ask them to come up with… wait for it… ideas! The fact that Pam from accounts could achieve the same thing by walking up to the boss and saying, 'I have an idea', should be ignored at all costs.

I lasted a full two weeks before it dawned on me that the surf could be up, there were records just begging to be found, and Charlie was at home on his rug thinking, *this blows!* I quit and hightailed it home, listening to one of my favourite albums of all time, Matt Finish's brilliant 'Short Note'.

Breathing a huge sigh of relief at escaping paid slavery forever, I cried tears of joy, knowing Charlie would be thinking the same thing I was when I hugged him. 'What were you thinking dickhead?'

Record/Chapter 50

ACDC — The Razors Edge (1990)

Brother From Another Planet

My earliest memory of my younger brother Craig (who this book is lovingly dedicated to), is of four-year-old me kissing his six-month-old chubby cheeks on a baby bouncer in the sun in the front yard in 1976. His chubby cheeks stayed with him his whole life. We nicknamed him Chubb, and even into young adulthood my other brother Michael and my parents and I would tease him, stealing kisses from his beautiful chubby cheeks.

Craig was an angel up until around age sixteen, when my parents made the unintentional mistake of letting him go to an agricultural boarding college in

Balclutha on the South Island of New Zealand. Surrounded by an assortment of primitive country bumpkins and delinquents, he quickly discovered pot, alcohol, sex, gambling, and importantly, how to use a radar detector to avoid the cops. It wasn't all bad though; every farmer's daughter wanted him, and he became the best sheep shearer in college history.

Fear didn't factor much in Craig's short life. He had an obsession with speed (thankfully not the drug), and whether it was a car, a motorbike, or a semi-trailer, he just couldn't help himself from finding out the absolute limits of anything mechanical he found himself behind the wheel of. This included any car that you were dumb enough to lend to him, which you would receive back with bald tyres, a grinding gearbox, or no brakes (on occasion all three).

Having said that, he was a brilliant driver, could reverse park a B-double semi-trailer on a dime, and could have held his own in a Formula One car if given the chance. I was always picking on him for his incessant speeding, but can't pretend I didn't get a boyish kick out of his skill at doing 'circle work' and smoking the tyres up at the lights.

Sadly, Craig found trouble a bit too easily throughout his life; or at least it found him. Alcohol played a part of course, as it does with many young men; but the sheer amount of dumb bad luck he encountered made us start to think God was playing a cruel joke on him.

In the early 2000s, Newcastle (Australia) saw a spate of terrible acts of random violence. One evening Craig must have looked at or said something to the wrong guy. He was kicked in the head so badly his jaw was not only broken but his chin bone was split in two. We visited him in the hospital, as he tried his best to drink soup with his head set in a cage of rods and pins.

A few months after his recovery, Craig was offered a job as a bus driver for the Contiki tour company in London; a dream job for any young guy. With his Leonardo DiCaprio-like looks and infectious smile, he no doubt looked forward to months of shagging his way around Europe (I mean, who wouldn't!). But on a night out, after blitzing the training, his drink was spiked with some kind of hallucinogenic drug. He spent day and night for a week wandering the streets of London in a daze, ending up in a psychiatric ward. Poor Mum had to fly to London to bring him home. Thankfully he made a full recovery after a few weeks living on another planet.

Then in 2008, while I was away working in the Solomon Islands, he suffered a horrific workplace injury that almost ended his life. At the time he was operations manager at a fertiliser plant in Newcastle. He made the mistake of jumping onto a moving conveyer belt in order to sweep off some leftover fertiliser. He slipped and fell, his arm becoming trapped at the point where the belt wrapped around a large piece of machinery. His arm was torn almost all the way off at the armpit. His saving grace was that he was a very solid, strong and big boned guy. If it was me in his place, my arm would now be gone. As his arm was being torn off, his adrenalin must have kicked in, as he managed to use his other arm to yank the mangled arm free. With his arm hanging on by a few pieces of muscle, his screams could be heard over a kilometre away.

His recovery and rehabilitation was extremely long and painful. The best surgeons in the country worked to save his arm, patching pieces of his leg and bottom into the huge gap that needed to be filled.

Although Craig and I were like chalk and cheese, and found each other unbearable at times, this horrible incident brought us closer than we had ever been as brothers. I walked with him to the local park, my arm around him as I cried my eyes out, thinking of the incomprehensible pain he would have endured. His accident reminded us how important family is, what a gift life is, and how fragile we all are. It also made me feel terribly guilty for all the times I had picked on him up to that point.

Craig's life wasn't all tragedy thankfully. He had the biggest heart you could imagine. His smile, his energy, and often even his simple presence, would light up any room. It's a well-worn cliché, but he would give the clothes off his back to help anyone in need, family, friend or stranger. He went above and beyond for his friends, even when some of them might not have deserved or even shown appreciation for his help. He had a lady killer smile, and cheekiness was part of his

DNA. His younger cousins loved him for his zest for life and his genuine interest and wonder in theirs.

Craig was larger than life. He could be loud, aggressive, painful, opinionated and exhausting (but then aren't we all at times?). Even having a fun conversation would leave you feeling like you'd just gone three rounds in a boxing ring. He was the proverbial bull in a china shop; but a bull with a huge heart, who, when all was said and done, just wanted those around him to be happy.

He was a big kid at heart, and into his thirties he would wake us up on Christmas morning at five a.m. to open all the presents. All his life he had a childlike wonder about the natural world, especially the ocean, which he spent a lot of time in and on. To help him fall asleep he would leave a David Attenborough documentary playing in the background.

One of my favourite moments with him was when we met up for a few days in Las Vegas. After he tested the limits of what a quad bike was capable of in the Nevada desert, we caught a Bee Gees tribute show. Side by side in the front row, Craig in a newly purchased pair of alligator skin cowboy boots (which he wore literally everywhere for the next few years), we pulled off our best *Saturday Night Fever* moves to 'You Should Be Dancing', singing at the top of our lungs while a room full of septuagenarians eyed us off.

Craig's claim to fame came when he appeared on the 'No Talent Time' segment of Australia's *Footy*

Show, singing ACDC's 'Thunderstruck'. One of his many talents was singing, and without a word of a lie, he could have easily stepped in for Brian Johnson (or Frank Sinatra for that matter). We have the tape; you have to see it to believe it!

My beautiful brother worked himself to death in the last years of his life. He loved his children Sonny and Ivy more than life itself. They were only four years and three months respectively at the time of his passing. Despite experiencing more tragedy and trouble than any man has a right to, I prefer to remember Craig for the joy he found in the simplest things. His infectious laugh and smile. His bear hug. His Mexican themed house parties. His ability to win over a stranger in minutes. His polite, gentle and caring nature. His bravery in tackling life's problems head on. His valuing of family above all else.

Nowadays I always shed a tear or two whenever I hear 'Thunderstruck' playing. But it also brings a smile, as I just know that Craig will be up in heaven, bugging Malcolm Young to accompany him on rhythm guitar, acting the showman as usual, and showering the family and friends up there with him with laughter and love. I miss you so much, brother. I hope you like my little book.